beach bach
boat barbecue

To Richard and Thelma
For your style, your artistry and creativity, and especially your cooking legacy

First published in 2001 by New Holland Publishers (NZ) Ltd
Auckland • Sydney • London • Cape Town

218 Lake Road, Northcote, Auckland, New Zealand
14 Aquatic Drive, Frenchs Forest, NSW 2086, Australia
86–88 Edgware Road, London W2 2EA, United Kingdom
80 McKenzie Street, Cape Town 8001, South Africa

www.newhollandpublishers.co.nz

Copyright © 2001 in text: Penny Oliver
Copyright © 2001 in photography: Ian Batchelor
Copyright © 2001 New Holland Publishers (NZ) Ltd

ISBN-13: 978 1 869660 24 6
ISBN-10: 1 869660 24 2

Managing editor: Matt Turner
Design: Christine Hansen
Editor: Alison Dench

A catalogue record for this book is available from the National Library of New Zealand

10 9 8 7 6

Colour reproduction by Pica Digital Pte Ltd, Singapore
Printed by Craft Print Pte Ltd, Singapore

All rights reserved. No part of this publication may be reproduced, stored in a retrieval system, or transmitted in any form or by any means, electronic, mechanical, photocopying, recording or otherwise, without the prior permission of the publishers and copyright holders.

The recipes in this book have been carefully tested by the author. The publishers and the author have made every effort to ensure that the recipes and the instructions pertaining to them are accurate and safe, but cannot accept liability for any resulting injury or loss or damage to property whether direct or consequential.

beach bach boat barbecue

Recipes by **Penny Oliver**

Photographs by **Ian Batchelor**

introduc

Many of us cherish special memories of summers past and I am no exception. I grew up in the deep south of New Zealand where people tend to be passionate about making the most of the abundant offerings that nature provides at that time of year. It was sacrilege if we couldn't have fresh peas, beans and new potatoes from the garden on Christmas Day (my father was a prolific grower and between his vegetable garden and my grandparents' we rarely lacked fresh supplies).

Back then, especially in the South Island, barbecues were not the regular event they tend to be for many people nowadays. However, one year we received a promising-looking package from my older sister in the United States. Naturally we younger kids fell upon it but we were well and truly baffled to find it full of a whole lot of metal bits and pieces. On close examination this metal collection revealed itself to be a kitset barbecue, which caused my father no end of consternation because he had no idea what to do with it. But that's another story...Messing about in boats, though, now that was a family trait. Every year, without fail, Dad used to sail in the Sanders Cup and we'd be there to cheer him on.

After Christmas the family would pack up all the necessary bits and pieces and head off to the beach or the river or the lake – the location varied because it all depended on who had lent us their bach that year. The one certainty was that we'd always take with us lots of seasonal produce – much of it procured en route at roadside honesty stalls. Once established in our temporary new territory, we'd quickly search out the best places to

forage for special treats – mussels, toheroa, berries – whatever could be gathered. The next few weeks were pure magic: the adults would lie back and enjoy a well-earned break and the children would utilise every moment between dawn and dusk, doing what children do.

My mother was no slouch in the kitchen, and her natural creativeness ensured food always looked sensational when it arrived at the table – whether this was at home or elsewhere. With this kind of heritage it's no surprise that by the age of four I was a dab hand at scrambled eggs and chives on doorstop toast, quickly graduating to gravy for the Sunday roast. Little wonder, really, that I grew up to become a food writer and food stylist.

And so given my background, the publication of this collection of ideas and recipes for the summer months – some of which date back to those idyllic times – seems a natural progression. Although divided into chapters for beach, bach, boat and barbecue, many of the recipes within these pages can be made wherever you are. Some are very simple and others are more challenging; I hope you will find them all tasty, accessible and user-friendly.

The recipes are influenced by a little nostalgia and the avant-garde flavours of the Pacific Rim and beyond. My aim is to allow the flavour of the food to speak for itself, without combining too many ingredients and thus disguising the food's natural flavours. Good food, after all, is about great taste.

beach

When I was a child every time my family set out in the car on a beach holiday we had a competition to see who could first spot the sea. The proud winner was entitled to say 'the poem', as we called it.

The sea, the sea
The open sea
The fresh, the blue
The ever free.
Without a mark, without a bound
It runs the world's wide regions round.

This ritual recitation signalled the true start of our beach holiday, banishing thoughts of school and replacing them with dreams of jumping waves, gathering mussels, swinging off pohutukawa trees and rolling down the sand dunes through the marram grass. I later worked

out the game was actually a clever parental ploy to make sure I, a bored back-seat passenger prone to motion sickness, kept my eye on the horizon. Strangely enough I had the keenest family eye and was always the first to burst into poetry.

The car groaned with produce packed into every cranny, isolated beach destinations being short on supermarkets at the time. One item received special attention – the old iron pot. Our large, heavy, black iron pot, with its lid, was the focus of much holiday fun and food. Daily, as the sun lowered, we gathered mussels, lit a fire amongst stones on the beach and feasted from the old iron pot. The sight and aroma of a steaming bowl of mussels still arouses for me nostalgia for childhood holidays.

The joy of preparing and eating simple, tasty food remains with me. Cooking and eating at the beach – be it nibbles between summer swims, a picnic with friends or an evening around the fire – demands simplicity. After all, being at the beach is all about serious relaxation and good slow eating.

Wood-roasted Salmon Tabbouleh

Smooth and rich in flavour, wood-roasted salmon partnered with textured burghul wheat makes a moist, moreish salad. Serve it with fresh pita bread.

1 1/2 cups burghul wheat
1/2 cup lemon juice
sea salt and freshly ground black pepper
4 spring onions, finely chopped
3/4 cup fresh flat-leaf parsley, chopped
1/2 cup fresh mint, chopped
1 telegraph cucumber, peeled, deseeded and chopped
2 large tomatoes, chopped
200g wood-roasted salmon, broken into pieces
1/4 cup extra virgin olive oil

Place the burghul wheat in a bowl and cover with cold water. Allow to soak for 1 hour, then drain. Transfer to a clean tea towel and thoroughly squeeze out all the remaining water. Combine the wheat, lemon juice, salt and pepper, spring onions, parsley, mint, cucumber, tomatoes and wood-roasted salmon. Drizzle the tabbouleh with the olive oil.

SERVES 4

Mussels with Fresh Tomato Sauce

Serve this dish piping hot with French bread to mop up the juice. The flavour gained by using fresh tomatoes rather than canned is well worth the effort, but if you are pressed for time you can use the basic Tomato Sauce recipe on page 126, halved.

3 tablespoons olive oil
1 small onion, peeled and finely chopped
2 cloves garlic, peeled and finely chopped
6 large tomatoes, skinned and coarsely chopped
2 tablespoons tomato paste
sea salt and freshly ground black pepper
pinch of sugar
3/4 cup fish stock (home-made or store-bought)
1/2 cup white wine
36 mussels, scrubbed and bearded
3 sprigs fresh thyme
extra thyme to garnish

In a saucepan sauté the olive oil, onion and garlic over a medium heat until soft. Add the chopped tomatoes and tomato paste and season to taste with salt, pepper and sugar. Add the fish stock and wine, then simmer until the tomatoes are slightly mushy and the sauce thickened. Drop in the mussels and fresh thyme sprigs, place a lid on the saucepan and cook for 3–4 minutes until the mussels open. Spoon the mussels and sauce into a serving bowl, garnish with more fresh thyme and serve immediately.

SERVES 4–6

Mussels with fresh tomato sauce

Chicken, Avocado and Pine Nut Fingers

The secret to these generous, moist, fat chicken sandwiches is the home-made mayonnaise.

1 store-bought barbecued chicken
1/2 cup toasted pine nuts
1 1/2 cups finely sliced celery
1 1/2 cups Basic Egg Mayonnaise (see page 78)
salt and freshly ground black pepper
softened butter for spreading
20 slices brown sandwich bread
1 firm ripe avocado, peeled and stoned
2 cups watercress and/or rocket leaves

Remove the skin from the chicken and discard. Remove the chicken meat from the carcass and cut it into bite-sized pieces. Combine the chicken, pine nuts, celery, mayonnaise and seasonings in a bowl until well mixed. Butter the bread and lay half the slices on a flat surface. Divide the chicken mixture between the 10 slices, spreading it evenly. Cut the avocado into thin slices and divide it between the sandwiches. Place a layer of watercress or rocket leaves over the avocado and top with the remaining buttered bread. Press down firmly, remove the crusts and cut each round into three fingers.

MAKES 30

Savoury Beach Frittatas

Quickly made with minimum fuss, these wonderful additions to the picnic basket are easily eaten wrapped in a crisp iceberg lettuce leaf.

8 eggs
2 cups cream
freshly ground black pepper
savoury flavouring (chopped crispy bacon or prosciutto; grated aged cheddar or parmesan cheese; crumbled feta or creamy blue cheese; freshly chopped basil, parsley, sage or thyme; diced cold roasted vegetables; flaked smoked fish; smoked or wood-roasted salmon; pesto, sun-dried tomatoes or tapenade)

Beat the eggs, cream and pepper together. Stir through your flavouring of choice. Pour the mixture into 1/2-cup capacity deep non-stick muffin pans, to three-quarters fill each pan. Bake in an oven preheated to 180°C for 20–25 minutes or until firm.

MAKES 12

Salmon, Roasted Red Pepper and Zucchini Pie

The buttery, tender short pastry is the making of this very tasty picnic pie. Serve it hot or cold.

PASTRY

250g (2 cups) plain flour, sifted
125g cold butter, cubed
pinch of salt
1 egg
1–2 teaspoons cold water

FILLING

180g streaky bacon, shredded
1 small red onion, peeled and finely chopped
1 clove garlic, peeled and finely chopped
1 red pepper (capsicum), roasted, skinned and deseeded (see page 124)
150g zucchini (courgettes), coarsely grated
sea salt and freshly ground black pepper
250g ricotta cheese
3/4 cup grated parmesan cheese
4 eggs, beaten
pinch of ground nutmeg
200g wood-roasted salmon

1 beaten egg to patch and glaze the pie

To make the pastry, place the flour, butter and salt in a food processor and process until the mixture resembles fine breadcrumbs. Add the egg and continue to process, adding enough cold water to bind the dough together. Remove the mixture to a lightly floured board and form the dough into a ball. Wrap in plastic wrap and refrigerate for 30 minutes.

To make the filling, fry the bacon over a low heat for 2 minutes. Add the onion and garlic and cook for 5 minutes or until soft. Cut the red pepper into strips. Squeeze any excess water from the zucchini and place in a bowl with the seasonings, ricotta, parmesan, beaten eggs, nutmeg and mix together.

On a lightly floured board roll out the pastry in a circle large enough to line a 23cm greased pie plate plus extra to fold over to cover the pie. Allow the excess dough to flop over the edge of the pie plate while you fill the pie. First spoon in the bacon mixture and spread it evenly over the pie base. Scatter the red pepper strips over. Spoon the zucchini mixture over. Break the salmon into small pieces and drop into the zucchini mixture. Fold the excess pastry over the pie and seal the edges. With a little beaten egg patch the pastry together on top, then prick or cut vents in the top of the pie. Brush the pie with the remaining egg wash. Bake in an oven preheated to 190°C for 40–45 minutes until cooked and golden. Allow the pie to cool, then cover with foil to pack in the picnic hamper.

SERVES 6–8

Salmon, roasted red pepper and zucchini pie

Summer Pizza

DOUGH

$^1/_4$ cup warm water
2 teaspoons dried yeast
pinch of sugar
1 cup warm water
3 tablespoons olive oil
pinch of salt
$2^3/_4$ cups plain flour

TOPPING

2 cups home-made Tomato Sauce (see page 126)
150g spicy pepperoni, sliced
8 artichoke hearts, sliced
1 cup black olives, stoned
150g feta cheese, crumbled
6 slices prosciutto, shredded
150g mozzarella cheese, thinly sliced
1 cup fresh basil, torn

To make the dough, place the first measure of warm water in a bowl and sprinkle the yeast and sugar over. Leave in a warm place until the mixture bubbles and becomes foamy. Add the second measure of warm water, the olive oil, salt and flour and mix together until it forms a dough. Transfer the dough to a lightly floured board. Knead until the dough is shiny, smooth and elastic. This should take 5–10 minutes. Place the dough in a lightly oiled bowl and cover with plastic wrap. Put the bowl in a warm place and allow the dough to rise and double its size. This takes 1–$1^1/_4$ hours. Knock down the dough and knead it into a smooth ball ready to use.

Divide the dough in half and roll out on a lightly floured board to make two pizza rounds. Spread the Tomato Sauce over the bases and arrange the remaining ingredients on top. Bake in an oven preheated to 220°C for 12–15 minutes.

SERVES 6

Pizza Bread

Pizza Bread is perfect served with Quick Antipasto Picks (see page 72).

Follow the instructions for making the dough for Summer Pizza (see opposite). Take the risen dough and roll it into an oblong shape about 2cm thick. Transfer it to a baking tray, brush with olive oil and leave plain or add flavour.

Salted Flat Bread: Brush with olive oil and sprinkle with sea salt.

Rosemary Flat Bread: Brush or spray with olive oil and sprinkle with fresh rosemary.

Olive Bread: Brush or spray with olive oil and sprinkle with $^1/_2$ cup slivered black olives.

Pesto Bread: Spread $^1/_2$ cup basil pesto over.

Sun-dried Tomato Bread: Spread $^1/_2$ cup sun-dried tomato paste over.

Bake in an oven preheated to 200°C for 20 minutes.

SERVES 8

Spinach, Chicken and Cheese Pie

1 onion, finely chopped
2 cloves garlic, peeled and crushed
25g butter
300g chicken breasts, thinly sliced
400g can tomatoes in juice, chopped
pinch of sugar
sea salt and freshly ground black pepper
400g store-bought flaky pastry
450g spinach, cooked, well drained and finely chopped
100g feta cheese, crumbled
1 egg yolk, beaten, for sealing and glazing

Gently fry the onion, garlic and butter together over a low heat until soft. Stir in the sliced chicken, tomatoes in juice, sugar, and salt and pepper. Gently simmer the chicken mixture for 15 minutes or until the chicken is cooked and the tomato is reduced to a thick paste. Set aside to cool.

On a floured board roll out the flaky pastry to an oblong of 40 x 30cm. Trim the edges with a sharp knife. Cut the oblong in half to form two halves 20 x 30cm, one for the base and one for the top. Place the bottom half on an oven tray. Fold the other sheet in half lengthways and cut through the folded edge with sharp scissors at 1cm intervals, leaving a 2cm border down the long side of the strip.

Brush the bottom sheet with the beaten egg yolk around the edge. Spread the chicken mixture over the middle of the pastry, leaving a 2cm border, and top this with the spinach then the feta. Carefully unfold the pastry top and place it over the filling. Press the edges of the pastry together and brush the pie with beaten egg yolk. Bake the pie in an oven preheated to 180°C for 20–30 minutes, until heated, golden brown and puffed.

SERVES 8

Spinach, chicken and cheese pie

Eggplant, Feta and Tomato Salad

This striking looking salad is equally striking to eat.

olive oil for spraying or brushing
2 eggplants (aubergines), thinly sliced
sea salt and freshly ground black pepper
6 tomatoes, sliced
150g cows milk feta cheese
1½ cups fresh mint
½ cup black Kalamata olives, stoned
½ red onion, peeled and finely sliced

DRESSING
¼ cup extra virgin olive oil
3–4 teaspoons lemon juice
sea salt and freshly ground black pepper

Spray or brush a couple of baking trays with olive oil. Place the eggplant slices on the trays in rows, spray or brush them with oil and season. Bake in an oven preheated to 200°C for 15 minutes or until golden brown. Turn and cook for a further 10 minutes. Layer the eggplant and tomato slices in a serving dish. Crumble the feta over, then sprinkle the mint, olives and onion on top.

To make the dressing, mix together the olive oil and lemon juice, and season. Drizzle the dressing over the salad and serve.

SERVES 8

Eggplant, feta and tomato salad

Pangritata and penne salad

Pangritata and Penne Salad

Pangritata, an Italian speciality, is simply breadcrumbs fried in garlic oil.

PANGRITATA
1/2 cup olive oil
2 cloves garlic, peeled and thinly sliced
1/4 cup fresh sage, shredded
3 cups fresh bread broken into bite-sized pieces
sea salt and freshly ground black pepper

1 1/2 cups dried penne
1/4 cup olive oil
6 sun-dried tomatoes, sliced
6 tomatoes, diced
150g mozzarella cheese, sliced
1 cup fresh basil
sea salt and freshly ground black pepper

To make the pangritata, heat the oil in a heavy-based frying pan over a medium–high heat. Add the garlic, sage and bread pieces and fry until the bread pieces are crisp and browned. Season to taste, drain on kitchen paper and keep warm.

Cook the penne in boiling salted water until al dente, then drain thoroughly. While the pasta is still warm, toss the olive oil, sun-dried and fresh tomatoes, mozzarella, fresh basil and pangritata through. Season to taste with salt and pepper.

SERVES 6–8

Prawn Salad

A light, versatile summer salad to serve on its own or packed into crusty rolls to take on a beach picnic. Try substituting the prawns with chicken, smoked chicken, salmon, tuna or crayfish.

4 cups cooked prawns, peeled
2 cups fresh watercress
1$^{1}/_{2}$ cups rocket leaves
3 oranges, peeled and segmented
2 tomatoes, coarsely chopped
1 small red onion, finely sliced
$^{1}/_{2}$ cup fresh mint
$^{1}/_{2}$ cup fresh basil

DRESSING
$^{1}/_{4}$ cup extra virgin olive oil
1 tablespoon lemon juice
$^{1}/_{4}$ cup sweet chilli sauce
dash of Tabasco sauce
sea salt and ground black pepper to taste

Place the prawns and the remaining salad ingredients in a bowl. To make the dressing, shake the ingredients together. Drizzle the dressing over the salad and gently toss together.

SERVES 6–8

Prawn salad in crusty rolls

Smoked Fish and Orzo with Fresh Herbs

Orzo, meaning 'barley' in Italian, is a tiny rice-shaped pasta about the size of a pine nut. It's great in soups, salads or as a substitute for rice. Serve this salad with a slice of pizza bread or roll it up in your favourite flat bread for easy packing in the picnic hamper.

$1\frac{1}{2}$ cups orzo pasta
$\frac{1}{4}$ cup extra virgin olive oil
olive oil for frying
120g baby spinach leaves, trimmed
$\frac{1}{3}$ cup fresh dill, chopped
$\frac{1}{3}$ cup chives, finely chopped
$\frac{1}{4}$ cup spring onions, finely sliced
$\frac{1}{4}$ cup fresh basil, finely shredded
$\frac{3}{4}$ cup fresh flat-leaf parsley, finely chopped
$\frac{1}{4}$ cup lemon juice
sea salt and freshly ground black pepper
200g smoked white fish, smoked eel or kabayaki dory, flaked

Cook the orzo in plenty of gently boiling water for 10–12 minutes or until al dente. Drain and rinse under running cold water, then drain again. Spoon into a serving bowl and toss with the olive oil until well coated. Heat a couple of tablespoons of olive oil in a large frying pan and wilt the spinach leaves. Add the spinach, dill, chives, spring onions, basil, parsley, lemon juice, salt and pepper, and fish to the orzo and gently toss together.

SERVES 4–6

Smoked fish and orzo with fresh herbs

Roast Shoulder of Lamb with Herb Anchovy Sauce

Sometimes called an oyster shoulder or a raised shoulder, this succulent, old-fashioned cut of lamb is the bone-in forequarter including the fore shank and shoulder blade. Roasted and allowed to cool it's a great hamper filler.

2 x 2kg oyster shoulders
12 cloves garlic, peeled and coarsely chopped
8 tablespoons fresh rosemary
4 tablespoons lemon juice
1/2 cup olive oil
freshly ground black pepper
6 tablespoons sea salt
1 1/2 cups Herb Anchovy Sauce (see below)

Use a sharp knife to score the surface of the lamb in a criss-cross pattern. To make the marinade, place the garlic, rosemary, lemon juice, olive oil and pepper in a food processor and pulse together to combine. Place the lamb in a shallow dish and paste the marinade over. Marinate for 1 hour, turning halfway through.

Place the shoulder and marinade in a roasting pan. Roast in an oven preheated to 200°C for 20 minutes. Sprinkle the salt over and roast for a further 30–35 minutes at 170°C until crusty and brown. Serve with a couple of dollops of Herb Anchovy Sauce on the side.

SERVES 8–10

Herb Anchovy Sauce

Aromatic and flavoursome, this punchy sauce will spark up roasted or grilled lamb, chicken or beef – and spread on bruschetta (see page 40) it's great as a nibble with drinks.

2 cups (packed) fresh flat-leaf parsley
1 1/4 cups (packed) fresh basil
1 cup (packed) fresh mint
2 cloves garlic, peeled
1 teaspoon capers, rinsed
2–3 anchovies
3–4 tablespoons red wine vinegar
6–8 tablespoons extra virgin olive oil
freshly ground black pepper
squeeze lemon juice
sea salt to taste

Roughly chop the parsley, basil and mint. Place all the ingredients in a food processor and blend to a thick sauce.

MAKES 1 1/2 CUPS

Ham and Herb Stuffed Chicken

Slice this roast chicken and serve it with a zingy relish on pizza bread for a satisfying picnic snack.

1 small onion, peeled and finely chopped
1 clove garlic, peeled and finely chopped
1 tablespoon olive oil
1 cup finely chopped leg ham
1 cup fresh white breadcrumbs
1/2 cup fresh flat-leaf parsley, finely chopped
2 tablespoons basil pesto (home-made or store-bought)
1 egg
sea salt and freshly ground black pepper
6 slices prosciutto
1 large chicken, boned

Fry the onion and garlic in the olive oil over a low heat until soft. Allow to cool, then add the ham, breadcrumbs, parsley, basil pesto, egg and seasoning. Stir well to combine. Line a 20cm long loaf tin with the prosciutto. Lay the chicken skin side down on a board. Place the stuffing in a sausage shape down the middle of the chicken, then fold the sides over. Place the chicken in the loaf tin folded side down, then fold the prosciutto over the top. Bake in an oven preheated to 180°C for 1 1/4–1 1/2 hours or until the juices run clear when a skewer is inserted. Allow to cool in the tin before removing and slicing.

SERVES 6–8

Sweet Sage Tomatoes

Sweet, sun-ripened tomatoes seasoned with sage complement lamb slices sandwiched in a crusty roll or a simple grilled sausage.

6 large tomatoes, halved
sea salt and freshly ground black pepper
2 cloves garlic, peeled and crushed
3 tablespoons olive oil
1 teaspoon honey
2 tablespoons balsamic vinegar
handful of fresh sage, shredded
extra olive oil
extra balsamic vinegar

Place the halved tomatoes cut side up in an ovenproof dish and season with salt and pepper. Shake together the garlic, olive oil, honey and balsamic vinegar and drizzle over the tomatoes. Sprinkle the sage on top, reserving a little for the garnish. Roast in an oven preheated to 150°C for 1 hour, until very soft and slightly charred. Sprinkle with extra shredded sage and drizzle with extra oil and vinegar to moisten.

SERVES 6

Sweet sage tomatoes

Apricot and Gingernut Fudge

This fudge is spicy, fruity and incredibly easy to make.

BASE
250g packet Gingernut biscuits
1/2 cup fresh walnuts, finely chopped
1/2 cup dried apricots, finely chopped
1 teaspoon ground ginger
100g butter
1/4 cup store-bought caramel condensed milk
1/4 cup brown sugar

ICING
1 1/2 cups icing sugar
1/2 teaspoon ground ginger
1 tablespoon melted butter
1 teaspoon grated orange zest
2 tablespoons orange juice
1/4 cup crystallised ginger, sliced

To make the base, crush the biscuits to fine crumbs, place in a bowl with the walnuts, apricots and ginger and stir together. Melt the butter with the condensed milk, then add the brown sugar and dissolve over a low heat. Add the condensed milk mixture to the biscuit crumb mixture, combine well and press into a shallow 26cm x 22cm baking tin.

To make the icing, sift the icing sugar and ground ginger into a bowl. Add the melted butter and orange zest and juice, and beat together until smooth. Spread evenly over the base, then sprinkle the crystallised ginger over. Refrigerate until firm, then cut into 40 fingers.

MAKES 40

Banana Carrot Cake

Sweet fruit and vegetable flavours give an old classic a new kick. It's delicious served with whipped cream.

1 cup plain flour
1 teaspoon baking powder
3/4 teaspoon baking soda
1/2 teaspoon salt
1/2 teaspoon ground cinnamon
3/4 cup brown sugar
1 teaspoon grated lemon zest
2 eggs
5 tablespoons vegetable oil
1 banana, mashed
1 cup grated carrot
1/4 cup pecans or hazelnuts

ICING
2 tablespoons melted butter
3 tablespoons soft cream cheese
grated zest of 1 lemon
1 teaspoon lemon juice
2 cups icing sugar, sifted

Butter and flour the sides of a 20cm cake tin. Sift the flour, baking powder, baking soda, salt and ground cinnamon into a bowl. Stir in the brown sugar and lemon zest. Add the eggs, oil and banana and combine. Add the carrot and nuts and mix well. Spoon into the prepared cake tin and bake in an oven preheated to 180°C for 35–40 minutes or until the cake springs back when pressed or a skewer comes out clean. Remove the cake from the tin and allow to cool on a wire rack.

To make the icing, beat the ingredients together until smooth. Spread over the top and sides of the cake.

SERVES 10

Sugared Orange and Almond Cakes

These are sticky, soft and very desirable treats.

125g butter, softened
2 teaspoons grated orange zest
1 cup caster sugar
4 eggs
2 cups ground almonds
1 cup self-raising flour
$^{1}/_{4}$ cup orange juice
$^{3}/_{4}$ cup sugar
whipped cream for serving

Beat the butter, orange zest and caster sugar in a bowl until light and creamy. Add the eggs one at a time, beating well after each addition. Lightly stir in the ground almonds and flour with a wooden spoon. Spoon the mixture to three-quarters fill twelve $^{1}/_{2}$-cup capacity greased or non-stick muffin pans. Bake in an oven preheated to 160°C for 20–25 minutes or until golden and an inserted skewer comes out clean. Remove the cakes from the pan while hot.

Combine the orange juice and sugar and spoon a little over each cake. Allow to stand for 3 minutes and serve warm with a dash of whipped cream.

Note: To make one big cake instead of 12 small ones, spoon the cake mixture into a greased and floured 20cm springform cake tin, then bake in an oven preheated to 170°C for 40 minutes or until an inserted skewer comes out clean.

MAKES 12

Sugared orange and almond cakes

Cherry and Almond Crumble Cake

150g blanched almonds
2 tablespoons plain flour
2 tablespoons oats
25g butter, softened
$^{1}/_{4}$ cup brown sugar
150g butter, softened
$^{3}/_{4}$ cup brown sugar (firmly packed)
3 eggs
$1^{2}/_{3}$ cups self-raising flour, sifted
1 teaspoon baking powder
1 teaspoon ground cinnamon
$1^{1}/_{2}$ cups cherries, stoned

Toast the almonds on a baking tray until lightly golden all over. Coarsely chop 25g of the almonds, grinding the remainder and setting them aside for the cake mixture. To make the topping, mix together the chopped almonds, flour, oats and the first measures of butter and brown sugar.

To make the cake, cream the second measures of butter and brown sugar until pale. Add the eggs one at a time, adding a little self-raising flour after each addition. Stir in the remaining flour, the baking powder, cinnamon and ground almonds. Spoon into a greased 25cm springform cake tin and smooth the top. Sprinkle the cherries evenly over the top of the cake and gently press them into the batter, then sprinkle the crumble topping over. Bake in an oven preheated to 180°C for 45–50 minutes or until an inserted skewer comes out clean. Allow the cake to cool for 10 minutes before removing from the tin, or transport to the picnic in the tin.

SERVES 8–10

bach

The bach in the north, the crib in the south – the New Zealand holiday house has come a long way from its beginnings more than a century ago, but in that time this traditionally humble dwelling with its basic plumbing, musty smell and damp mattresses has earned the rank of official Kiwi icon right next to the Buzzy Bee. The modern designer bach is a different animal but most still apply the fundamental bach philosophy – they take in the view, are open plan and have indoor/outdoor living.

Whether it's in an architect's dream by a lake or a Fibrolite in the dunes, though, we're all there for the same reason: respite from the domestic grind. At the bach there's time – time to dawdle, time to relax, and time to indulge in favourite recipes for long, leisurely meals with family and friends.

As a child I holidayed at my best friend's family bach in the hills of Central Otago. There we were allowed a wonderful freedom. Time was forgotten as we cooled down in the Clutha's swimming holes and scrambled over the rocky thyme- and rosehip-covered hills. We whiled away the hours damming and redirecting small streams, panning for gold and availing ourselves, uninvited, of tree-ripened stone fruits at local orchards.

The bach was quite exotic for its day. Built into the hillside from local stone, it had doors and windows that opened on one side to staggered stone terraces overlooking the river. The large, open, riverstone-clad fireplace was fascinating, reminding me of an American mountain cabin. Best of all was the bunkroom where we happily retired, weary and singed by the sun, to spook ourselves to sleep with creepy stories and plans to raid the fridge of leftover pavlova at midnight.

Bruschetta

With some smoky grilled bread and a couple of quickly made relishes on hand, tasty pre-dinner morsels are a breeze.

ciabatta or country-style bread
olive oil for spraying

Cut the bread into 1cm slices and spray both sides with olive oil. Cook on the barbecue grill for a couple of minutes each side until golden but still tender.

TOP WITH:
- Wood-roasted Salmon with Black Olive Dressing
- Cows milk feta cheese, fromage blanc or quark with Red Chilli and Pepper Relish (see page 42)
- Prosciutto, shaved ham or thinly sliced rare beef with Beetroot and Apple Relish (see page 42) and horseradish cream

Wood-roasted Salmon with Black Olive Dressing

1/2 telegraph cucumber, skinned and chopped
100g cows milk feta cheese, crumbled
200g grilled artichoke hearts, sliced
200g wood-roasted salmon, broken into small pieces
freshly ground black pepper

BLACK OLIVE DRESSING
1/3 cup black olives, stoned
2 1/2 tablespoons lemon juice
1/4–1/3 cup extra virgin olive oil
sea salt and freshly ground black pepper

Place the cucumber, feta, artichoke hearts, salmon and pepper in a bowl and gently mix together. To make the dressing, blend all the ingredients together in a food processor, using enough olive oil to make a thick paste.

Pile the salmon mixture onto the bruschetta and top with a little Black Olive Dressing.

SERVES 10

Bruschetta

Beetroot and Apple Relish

800g fresh beetroot, peeled and coarsely grated
1 large onion, peeled and finely chopped
350g green apples, peeled, cored and finely chopped
1 cup white wine vinegar
$^2/_3$ cup balsamic vinegar
1 cup brown sugar
2 tablespoons lemon juice
1 teaspoon Dijon mustard
salt

Place all the ingredients in a large heavy-based saucepan and stir over a low heat until the sugar dissolves. Bring to the boil and simmer, stirring occasionally, for 30 minutes or until the mixture is tender and thick. Spoon into warm, clean jars, seal and store in a cool, dark place. After opening it will keep in the refrigerator for up to six weeks.

MAKES 4 CUPS

Red Chilli and Pepper Relish

This deliciously biting relish is a quick way to add zing to meals over summer.

4 large red peppers (capsicums)
2 onions, peeled and coarsely chopped
1 large fresh red chilli, deseeded
3 cloves garlic, peeled
2 cups white wine vinegar
approximately 780g sugar
salt
2 kaffir lime leaves
1 bay leaf

Slice around the core of the red peppers, remove any white membrane and roughly chop. In batches place the red peppers, onions, chilli and garlic in a food processor and pulse until smooth. Transfer to a heavy-based saucepan. Add the vinegar and simmer for 20 minutes.

Pour the mixture into a measuring jug to establish the quantity made. Add an equal amount of sugar and return both to the saucepan. Stir until the sugar dissolves, then return to a gentle boil. Season to taste with salt, and add the kaffir lime leaves and bay leaf. Stir occasionally.

Remove the scum with a metal spoon as it simmers for 30 minutes or until it looks thick. Remove the kaffir lime and bay leaves. Spoon the relish into warm, clean jars, seal and store in a cool, dark place for up to a year. After opening it will keep in the refrigerator for up to six weeks.

MAKES 5 CUPS

Whitebait Fritters

The delicate flavour of whitebait is captured in these generous, plump fritters. Serve them simply with lemon wedges and your favourite bread.

4 tablespoons plain flour
1/4 teaspoon baking soda
pinch of salt
4 eggs, separated
4 tablespoons milk
grated zest of 1 lemon
freshly ground black pepper
400–500g fresh whitebait, rinsed under cold water and well drained
olive oil for cooking

Place the flour, baking soda and salt in a bowl and make a well in the centre. Beat the egg yolks and milk together, then stir the lemon zest and pepper in. Pour the egg mixture into the dry ingredients and beat with a whisk until the batter is smooth. Add the whitebait and combine. Beat the egg whites until they form stiff peaks.

Just before cooking, fold the egg whites into the whitebait batter. Thinly cover the bottom of a heavy-based frying pan with olive oil and heat to medium–high. Drop spoonfuls of mixture into the hot oil three or four at a time and cook until the underside is golden. Turn and cook the other side until the fritters are just set.

MAKES 14–16

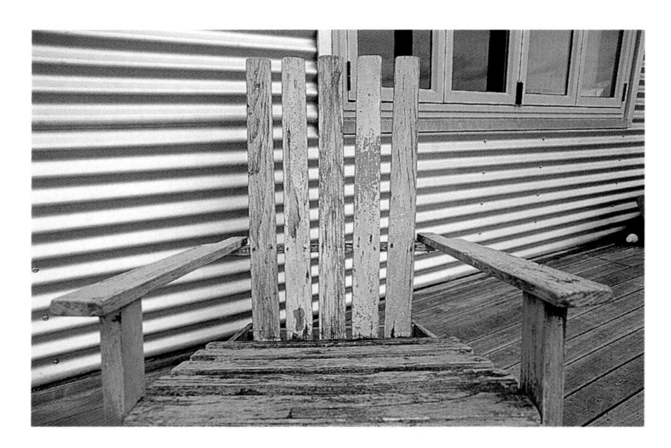

Whitebait fritters

Tomato, Bacon and Pasta Frittata

A soft, eggy frittata with a crisp summer salad and crusty bread creates a perfect holiday lunch. As a variation try using pancetta or prosciutto in place of bacon, or cooked potato in place of penne.

2 tablespoons olive oil
1 small onion, finely chopped
$^{1}/_{2}$ cup finely chopped bacon
100g cherry tomatoes, halved
6 eggs
100g parmigiano-reggiano cheese, grated
$^{1}/_{4}$ cup milk
$^{1}/_{4}$ cup cream
$^{1}/_{2}$ cup fresh flat-leaf parsley and fresh basil, mixed
freshly ground black pepper
200g penne, cooked al dente

Heat the olive oil in a large frying pan and cook the onion and bacon over a low heat for 2 minutes. Add the tomatoes and cook for a further 5 minutes. Allow to cool. Combine the eggs, cheese, milk, cream and herbs and whisk together. Add the tomato mixture, pepper and penne and stir together. Spoon the mixture into a 23cm springform pan with the base lined with well-oiled aluminium foil. Place on a baking tray in an oven preheated to 190°C for 30 minutes or until the frittata is risen, golden and just set. Allow to cool for 10 minutes in the tin before removing.

SERVES 6–8

Ricotta and Fresh Asparagus Crêpes

These crêpes look and taste just great. You can serve them warm or cold; try them with a little Roasted Red Pepper Mayonnaise (see page 124) on the side.

$1^{1}/_{2}$ cups plain flour
1 egg
3 egg yolks
600ml milk
olive oil for frying
350g ricotta cheese
50g cows milk feta cheese
grated zest of 1 lemon
$^{1}/_{2}$ tablespoon lemon juice
freshly ground black pepper
16 fine slices prosciutto
approximately 36 fresh asparagus spears, trimmed and blanched
120g rocket leaves or salad greens

To make the crêpe mixture, place the flour in a bowl and make a well in the centre. In a separate bowl beat the egg, egg yolks and milk together. Gradually pour the liquid into the well, whisking continuously until it forms a batter. Cover and allow to stand at room temperature for 30 minutes.

To make the filling, beat the ricotta and feta cheese, lemon zest and juice, and pepper together until smooth. Spray a 17cm frying pan with olive oil and place on a medium heat. Make crêpes using about $^{1}/_{4}$ cup of crêpe mixture at a time and set aside.

Spread each crêpe with a spoonful of ricotta mixture. To one side of the crêpe lay down a slice of prosciutto. Lay 3 asparagus spears on top, then a sprinkling of rocket leaves. Roll up the crêpe and serve.

MAKES 10–12

Eggplant and Wood-roasted Salmon Wraps

2 large eggplants (aubergines)
olive oil for cooking
300g fromage blanc or quark
400g wood-roasted salmon
freshly ground black pepper
lemon juice to taste
200g rocket leaves
$^1/_4$ cup dukkah

Trim the ends from the eggplants and slice each lengthways into six to eight 5mm slices. Cover the bottom of a frying pan with olive oil. Over a medium–high heat fry the slices of eggplant until golden brown on both sides, adding more oil as required. Drain the eggplant slices on absorbent kitchen paper and allow to cool.

Lay the eggplant slices out on a flat surface and spread each evenly with a thin layer of fromage blanc or quark. Top each slice with 25g salmon. Add pepper and a squeeze of lemon juice to taste. Place a small handful of rocket leaves across one end of each slice and roll up. Lay the rolls in a serving dish and top with a sprinkle of dukkah. Serve immediately.

MAKES 12–16

Eggplant and wood-roasted salmon wraps

Asian Beef Salad

Thai flavours mix and meld in a light, fragrant salad just right for a hot summer's day. Serve it in individual bowls as a starter or as part of a main meal.

2 cloves garlic, peeled and crushed
2 tablespoons sesame oil
2 tablespoons fish sauce
1 tablespoon hot chilli sauce
2 tablespoons soy sauce
2 kaffir lime leaves, shredded
500g piece of scotch fillet, trimmed
150g uncooked vermicelli noodles
1/2 telegraph cucumber, peeled
3 shallots (eschallots), peeled and finely chopped
1/4 cup (packed) fresh mint, shredded
1/4 cup (packed) fresh coriander
1/4 cup (packed) fresh basil
1 cup crisp salad greens (mesclun or rocket)

DRESSING
1 fresh red chilli, deseeded and finely chopped
1 clove garlic, peeled and crushed
1/4 cup lime juice
1–2 tablespoons fish sauce
2 tablespoons grated palm sugar
1 tablespoon sesame oil

To make the marinade, shake together in a jar the garlic, sesame oil, fish sauce, hot chilli sauce, soy sauce and kaffir lime leaves. Place the beef in a dish just large enough to snugly contain it and pour the marinade over. Turn the beef to give it a good coating, then marinate for 30 minutes.

Sear the beef on a oiled grill or barbecue over a high heat. Transfer to a roasting pan and cook in an oven preheated to 200°C for 20–25 minutes. Cover the meat with aluminium foil and allow to rest for 30 minutes, then slice finely.

Place the noodles in a bowl, cover with boiling water and allow to stand for 5 minutes. Rinse the noodles in cold water and drain well. Roughly cut them to a manageable length with scissors. Cut the cucumber in half lengthways, core and chop finely. Place the noodles, cucumber, shallots, mint, coriander, basil and salad leaves in a serving platter. Shake the dressing ingredients together and pour half over the noodles and salad and gently toss. Arrange the sliced beef over and around the salad. Drizzle over the remaining dressing and combine.

SERVES 6–8

Warm Lamb Salad

1 red pepper (capsicum), roasted, skinned and deseeded (see page 124)
$^1/_2$ cup black olives, stoned
2–3 cups salad greens
2–3 cups rocket leaves
2 cups torn pieces of crusty bread
4 tablespoons olive oil for frying
600g lamb backstrap
$^1/_2$ cup balsamic vinegar
2 tablespoons lemon juice
sea salt and freshly ground black pepper
shaved parmesan cheese for serving

Slice the red pepper into thin strips and place in a bowl with the olives, salad greens and rocket leaves. Put aside in a cool place. Fry the torn bread pieces in the olive oil until crisp and golden, then drain on absorbent kitchen paper and put aside. Add the lamb to the frying pan and brown it over a high heat for 4–5 minutes on each side. Allow the lamb to rest for 10 minutes, then slice it.

Gently toss the red pepper, olives and greens together and arrange on a serving platter. Reheat the lamb pan and pour the balsamic vinegar and lemon juice into it. Season with salt and pepper and simmer for 2–3 minutes. Place the crisp bread and sliced lamb amongst the salad and drizzle the dressing over. Top with shaved parmesan.

SERVES 6–8

Roast Duck Salad with Verjuice Dressing

Verjuice is simply the juice made from unripe grapes. If you can't find it in your local speciality store, you can use white wine vinegar instead. For the salad greens in this recipe I use a mixture of rocket, watercress and cos lettuce.

2 ducks or 4 duck breasts, roasted
1 red onion, peeled, halved and finely sliced
6 spring onions, cut in 2cm lengths
1 firm, ripe mango, peeled and finely sliced
1 cup croûtons
1 cup unsalted cashew nuts, toasted
2 cups salad greens
Verjuice Dressing (see below)

Remove the skin and flesh from the duck and slice the meat into bite-sized pieces. In a large bowl toss together the duck, red onion, spring onions, mango, croûtons, cashew nuts and salad greens. Just before serving, drizzle over enough Verjuice Dressing to moisten the salad. Spoon into a serving dish and serve immediately.

SERVES 6–8

Verjuice Dressing

1 clove garlic, peeled and crushed
1/4 cup extra virgin olive oil
1/2 cup white verjuice
1/4 cup orange juice
1 tablespoon grated palm sugar
1 kaffir lime leaf, finely shredded
1 fresh red chilli, deseeded and finely chopped

Shake all the ingredients together in a jar 1 hour before using.

MAKES 1 CUP

Chargrilled Vegetable Salad

2 red peppers (capsicums)
2 yellow peppers (capsicums)
6–8 asparagus spears, cut in half lengthways and blanched
4 zucchini (courgettes), ends trimmed
2 red onions, peeled
300g button mushrooms
olive oil for brushing or spraying
1/4 cup fresh basil, torn

DRESSING
4 tablespoons extra virgin olive oil
3 tablespoons balsamic vinegar
sea salt
2 tablespoons lemon juice

To prepare the vegetables, halve the peppers and remove the seeds and membrane. Place cut side down on a grill tray and cook under a hot grill until they char and the skins blister. Allow to cool, then peel and cut into bite-sized pieces. While the peppers cool cut the zucchini into quarters lengthways. Cut the red onions into eighths, leaving the root end on to keep the onion intact. Place the asparagus, zucchini, mushrooms and onions on a lightly oiled grill tray. Brush or spray the vegetables with olive oil and cook under a hot grill until the vegetables are slightly charred and softened. Gently toss the grilled vegetables with the dressing and spoon into a serving dish. Scatter the torn basil over the salad.

To make the dressing, combine the ingredients.

SERVES 6–8

Chargrilled vegetable salad

Pacific Prawns and Kumara Cakes

700g green prawns, peeled and deveined with tails intact
2 cloves garlic, peeled and crushed
grated zest of 1 lime
2 tablespoons lime juice
1 teaspoon grated fresh ginger
1 tablespoon hot chilli sauce
1/4 cup coconut milk
2 tablespoons fresh coriander, chopped
lemon wedges to garnish

KUMARA CAKES
250g golden kumara (sweet potatoes), peeled and coarsely grated
250g zucchini (courgettes), coarsely grated
2 tablespoons fresh coriander, chopped
pinch of ground nutmeg to taste
freshly ground black pepper
grated zest of 1 lemon
1 1/4 cups cooked short-grain rice
1/4 cup self-raising flour
1 egg
peanut oil for frying

Combine the prawns with the garlic, lime zest and juice, ginger, chilli sauce, coconut milk and coriander, gently stirring to ensure the prawns are well coated. Cover and refrigerate until needed.

To make the Kumara Cakes, put the ingredients in a bowl and mix together well. Divide the mixture into 8–10 portions and shape into small cakes. Fry the cakes in a little peanut oil over a medium–high heat, allowing them to thoroughly crisp on one side before you turn them.

Cook the prawns on a lightly oiled grill until the flesh just whitens. Serve 6–8 prawns on top of each of the Kumara Cakes, with a wedge of lemon on the side.

SERVES 8

Potato and Prosciutto Salad

It's important to use good quality new potatoes in a potato salad . . . I find Jersey Bennes are perfect.

2 cloves garlic, peeled and crushed
1/4 cup fresh dill
1/4 cup fresh basil
1/4 cup fresh sage
1/4 cup fresh flat-leaf parsley
3 spring onions, sliced
1/4–1/2 cup extra virgin olive oil
sea salt
24 small new potatoes, washed
12 slices prosciutto, grilled crisp

To make the dressing, place the garlic, herbs and spring onions in a food processor. With the motor running drizzle in enough olive oil to form a medium–thick dressing. Season with salt. Scrape the potatoes to remove the skins, boil until tender and drain. Break the prosciutto into pieces. Pile the potatoes and prosciutto on a serving platter and drizzle the dressing over.

SERVES 6

Beetroot Salad

600g beetroot, trimmed, peeled and cut into wedges
olive oil for roasting
1 red onion, peeled, halved and sliced
1 clove garlic, peeled and crushed
olive oil for frying
sea salt and freshly ground black pepper
2 tablespoons balsamic vinegar
1/3 cup orange juice
1 cup cherry tomatoes, halved
150g cows milk feta cheese (optional)
1/2 cup fresh flat-leaf parsley, chopped
1/2 cup fresh mint, shredded

Place the beetroot in a roasting pan and drizzle with a little olive oil to moisten. Roast in an oven preheated to 200°C for 30 minutes or until tender. While the beetroot is roasting, fry the onion and garlic in a little olive oil over a gentle heat until tender. Season with salt and pepper, and set aside.

When the beetroot is ready, drain the juice from the beetroot into the pan of onion and garlic. Place the beetroot wedges in a serving bowl. Reheat the onion mixture over a high heat. Add the balsamic vinegar and orange juice and simmer for 2 minutes. Remove from the heat. When the mixture stops boiling pour it over the beetroot wedges. Scatter the tomatoes over the beets and crumble the feta on top. Garnish with the parsley and mint.

SERVES 6–8

Pot-roasted Lemon and Thyme Chicken

When serving this dish cold, remove the chicken and juices from the cooking pot to a serving dish, allow it to cool, then refrigerate it until the juices gel around the meat.

1.3kg corn-fed chicken
1 lemon, halved
5 sprigs fresh thyme
4 cloves garlic, peeled
50g butter
$^{1}/_{2}$ cup fresh flat-leaf parsley
2 tablespoons lemon juice
$^{1}/_{4}$ cup olive oil
sea salt and freshly ground black pepper
100ml Riesling
$^{1}/_{2}$ lemon, finely sliced
2 bay leaves
extra 3 sprigs fresh thyme

Thoroughly dry the chicken with absorbent kitchen paper and cut two slashes into the thick flesh of each chicken leg. Stuff the chicken cavity with the lemon halves and sprigs of fresh thyme. Place the garlic, butter and parsley in a food processor or blender and pulse together. With the motor still running add the lemon juice and olive oil and blend to a spreadable paste.

Ease a little paste underneath the skin on each breast and rub the remaining paste over the chicken. Place in a casserole dish or ovenproof pot with a lid. Season and pour in the Riesling. Place the lemon slices, bay leaves and extra thyme over and around the chicken. Cover the dish with a firm lid and roast the chicken in an oven preheated to 190°C for 1$^{1}/_{2}$ hours or until the juices run clear when a skewer is inserted. Baste during cooking. If you like a brown chicken remove the lid for the last 30 minutes of cooking. If serving hot, allow the chicken to rest for 15 minutes before carving.

SERVES 4–6

Red Curry Chicken Mayonnaise

This moist chicken salad recipe gives tried and true Coronation Chicken a new lease of life. It's delicious spooned into split French bread and put in the picnic hamper.

1 onion, peeled and finely chopped
1 tablespoon olive oil
2 teaspoons Thai red curry paste
1 cup chicken stock
2 tablespoons tomato paste
2 tablespoons dry sherry
1 tablespoon lemon juice
$^{3}/_{4}$ cup apricot jam
2$^{1}/_{2}$ cups Basic Egg Mayonnaise (see page 78)
2 chickens, boiled until tender
1 cup celery, finely sliced
$^{1}/_{4}$ cup pine nuts, toasted
watercress sprigs for serving

Gently fry the onion in the olive oil over a low heat until soft. Add the curry paste, stock, tomato paste, sherry, lemon juice and apricot jam and whisk together. Simmer, uncovered, for 10 minutes, then allow to cool.

Add the mayonnaise to the curry mixture and combine. Discard the chicken skin and remove the meat from the carcass. Cut the chicken into bite-sized pieces. Mix together the chicken, celery and mayonnaise mixture until the chicken is lightly coated. Spoon into a serving dish and finish the top with the pine nuts and watercress.

SERVES 10–12

Stock-poached Beef

Cooled and thinly carved, this tasty dish is a handy back-up when catering for visiting crowds.

2 x 800g pieces scotch fillet
3 cups veal or beef stock
3 cups chicken stock
2 bay leaves
3 sprigs fresh thyme

Trim the scotch fillet of excess fat and sinew and tie at four 4cm intervals with string to form a neat shape. Refrigerate for 1 hour. Place the beef in the bottom of a saucepan just big enough to snugly fit the meat. Pour in enough stock to cover the meat. Add the herbs, cover with a lid and bring to the boil. For rare meat, poach gently for 20 minutes. Remove from the saucepan and allow to rest for 10–15 minutes before carving.

SERVES 10–12

Roasted Red Onion, Raisins and Pine Nuts

This tangy dish is particularly good served with poached or grilled meat.

1kg red onions
1/3 cup extra virgin olive oil
1/2 cup balsamic vinegar
1/4 cup raisins
1/4 cup pine nuts

Peel the onions and cut into eighths, leaving enough of the root end intact that the onions don't come apart. Place in one layer in a roasting tin. Pour the olive oil and balsamic vinegar over. Cover with aluminium foil and cook in an oven preheated to 200°C for 25 minutes. Remove the foil and sprinkle in the raisins and pine nuts. Cook for a further 15–20 minutes, until the onions are soft, the raisins plump and the pine nuts slightly brown.

SERVES 6

Stock-poached beef with roasted red onion,
raisins and pine nuts

Spiced Roast Lamb

Roasted meats are a huge, no-fuss asset over the summer months. Serve Spiced Roast Lamb hot or cold, accompanied with a tangy relish, salad or grilled vegetables, or in sandwiches.

1.5kg leg of lamb
4 cloves garlic, peeled
1/4 cup fresh mint
1/4 cup fresh coriander
1/4 cup fresh flat-leaf parsley
2 teaspoons ground cumin
sea salt and freshly ground black pepper
1/4 cup olive oil

Using a sharp knife score the surface of both sides of the lamb 5–10mm deep in a criss-cross pattern. Place the garlic, mint, coriander, parsley, cumin and seasonings in a blender or food processor. Pulse to combine. Drizzle in the olive oil while the processor runs and mix to a thick, spreadable paste. Spread the paste over both sides of the lamb and work it into the cut surfaces with your hands. Loosely cover the lamb and set aside in a cool place for an hour. Roast the lamb in an oven preheated to 190–200°C for about 1 1/4 hours. This achieves a cooked outer flesh and slightly pink inside. Allow to rest for 15 minutes before carving or serve cold.

SERVES 6–8

Summer Trifle

The decadence of the rich trifle is set off by the essence of summer – raspberries.

1 cup cold strong espresso coffee
1/2 cup crème de cassis
250g packet Italian sponge fingers
2 cups mascarpone cheese
1/2 cup cream
1/4 cup icing sugar
2 eggs
1/3 cup caster sugar
100g dark cooking chocolate, melted
2 1/2 –3 cups fresh raspberries
icing sugar for serving

Combine the coffee and half the crème de cassis in a shallow bowl. Dip half the packet of sponge fingers in the coffee mixture one or two at a time and cover the bottom of an 8-cup capacity flat-bottomed serving dish. Reserve the remaining coffee mixture. In a bowl combine the remaining crème de cassis and the mascarpone and set aside. Beat the cream and icing sugar together until thick. Fold this mixture into the mascarpone mixture. Beat the eggs and caster sugar together until thick and fluffy and fold into the mascarpone mixture. Divide this mixture in half. Fold the melted chocolate through half of this mixture.

Pour the chocolate mascarpone mixture over the sponge finger base. Sprinkle over half the raspberries. Dip the remaining biscuits in the coffee mixture and layer on top of the raspberries. Pour the remaining mascarpone mixture over and top with the remaining fresh raspberries to completely cover the top. Refrigerate for at least 4 hours, preferably overnight. To serve finish the top with a little icing sugar and serve at room temperature.

SERVES 8

Chocolate Raspberry Pavlovas

This truly spectacular dessert is best assembled 20 minutes before it is served. You can make the pavlovas ahead of time and store them in an airtight container.

PAVLOVAS

1 cup ground almonds
$^1/_3$ cup cocoa powder, sifted
2 tablespoons cornflour, sifted
6 egg whites
pinch of salt
$^1/_2$ teaspoon cream of tartar
$1^1/_2$ cups caster sugar

MASCARPONE CREAM

300g mascarpone cheese
100ml cream, lightly whipped
2 tablespoons caster sugar

CHOCOLATE SAUCE

100g dark cooking chocolate
120ml cream

RASPBERRY SAUCE

$^1/_2$ cup raspberries
3 tablespoons caster sugar
2 teaspoons water

TO ASSEMBLE

200ml cream, whipped
2 cups raspberries
2 tablespoons ground almonds, toasted golden

Line two baking trays with non-stick baking paper. In a bowl combine the ground almonds, cocoa and cornflour. In another bowl beat the egg whites, salt and cream of tartar together until they form soft peaks. Gradually add the caster sugar while beating the egg whites until they are thick, shiny and stiff. Add a third of the almond mixture to the egg whites and fold in. Fold in the remaining two-thirds of the almond mixture.

Take approximately $^1/_2$ cup of mixture and place it on a lined baking tray. Shape the mixture into small square shapes with a flat top. Repeat the process with the remaining mixture, spacing the squares well. Bake in an oven preheated to 100°C for 45 minutes. Turn off the oven and leave the pavlovas to cook in the oven.

To make the Mascarpone Cream, combine the mascarpone with the whipped cream and caster sugar. To make the Chocolate Sauce, melt the chocolate and cream together. To make the Raspberry Sauce, gently simmer the raspberries with the caster sugar and water until the sugar dissolves and the fruit softens, then mash with a fork.

To assemble, place each pavlova on a serving plate and drizzle it with Chocolate Sauce. Top with a dollop of Mascarpone Cream, some whipped cream and a little Raspberry Sauce and finish with fresh raspberries and a sprinkle of toasted almonds.

MAKES 10–12

Apricot and Polenta Shortcake

This simple shortcake keeps well and is a great standby for unexpected guests.

350g fresh apricots, halved and stones removed
1/4 cup water
1/4 cup sugar
150g polenta
125g plain flour
120g ground almonds
3/4 teaspoon baking powder
150g caster sugar
150g butter, softened
1/2 teaspoon ground cinnamon
1 egg, beaten
icing sugar for serving
vanilla sugared whipped cream for serving

Heat the apricots, water and sugar together in a saucepan over a medium heat, stirring to dissolve the sugar before it comes to the boil. Simmer for 5–10 minutes or until the apricots are tender. Allow to cool.

Place the polenta, flour, ground almonds, baking powder, sugar and butter in a food processor. Process the mixture until it resembles coarse breadcrumbs. Add the cinnamon and egg. Continue to process until the mixture forms a dough. Remove the dough from the food processor and divide in half. Line a 25cm x 18cm baking tin with greased baking paper. Press one half of the dough evenly over the bottom of the tin and spread the apricot mixture over the base. Dot the remaining dough in chunks on the top and gently press it together. Bake in an oven preheated to 180°C for 40–45 minutes or until golden. Dredge the top with icing sugar and serve with a dollop of vanilla sugared whipped cream.

SERVES 8–10

Vanilla Sugar

Stir this flavoured sugar through whipped cream or sprinkle it over fresh berries to give a great shot of vanilla.

2 fresh, moist vanilla pods
500g caster sugar

Cut the vanilla pods into small pieces. Place the pods and sugar in a food processor and pulse together until the sugar is ash coloured. Sieve the mixture, return the lumps to the food processor, pulse again and add them to the rest of the sugar. Store in an airtight container.

MAKES 2 CUPS

Brownies and Berries

Chocoholics will delight in these rich brownies tempered by fresh seasonal berries.

60g dark cooking chocolate, broken into pieces
125g unsalted butter
2 eggs
1 cup caster sugar
2 tablespoons cocoa powder
2 tablespoons golden syrup
1/2 cup ground almonds
1/4 cup plain flour, sifted
1/2 cup sour cream
3/4 cup blanched almonds, coarsely chopped

CHOCOLATE GANACHE
100g dark cooking chocolate
100ml cream

3 cups mixed summer berries

Melt the chocolate and butter together in a heavy-based saucepan over a very low heat or microwave on low power. Allow to cool slightly. In a bowl beat the eggs and sugar together until pale and creamy. Slowly beat in the chocolate mixture, cocoa and golden syrup. Add the ground almonds and flour in two batches, beating well after each addition. Fold in the sour cream and blanched almonds. Spoon into a lightly greased 20cm x 25cm brownie or slice tin. Bake in an oven preheated to 170°C for 30–35 minutes. Allow to cool in the pan, then cover with Chocolate Ganache and refrigerate for 1 hour. Cut into squares and serve.

To make the Chocolate Ganache, break the chocolate into pieces. Pour in the cream and melt the ingredients together until smooth.

MAKES 16–18

Brownies and berries

boat

It is hardly surprising, given New Zealand is dotted with lakes and rivers and surrounded by sea, that so many Kiwis love to mess about in boats. The regular summer sight of a marina half empty is evidence of our romance with the sea, whether it takes the form of a day out fishing in a dinghy or a couple of weeks cruising the islands and bays of our coastline.

Yachting is the ultimate in laid-back holidays. Days begin at a leisurely pace: don the togs for a quiet dip off the back of the boat, dry off in the sun, then add a hat, a slather of sunscreen and a beach wrap – bingo, dressed for the day.

First one up starts the coffee and 'brekky'. Fellow boaties surface slowly to attend this critical meal where the key decision is: do we stay put or fish or sail? Fishing is an attractive prospect: the

idea of a fresh catch to barbecue that evening is mouth-watering. Appetites grow at sea and throughout the day, as hunger and thirst strike, platters of juicy, moist snacks and trays of drinks are required to appease ravenous boaties.

As the afternoon slips away there is time for another swim and a laze in the shade of the sails. Exhausted from the day of sun, sea and salt, family and friends find a stiff sundowner revives both the spirit and the appetite. Some recently harvested mussels with grilled herbs seem perfect to start the evening meal, with crisp roasted snapper to follow.

At the end of a long day, in the shelter of the bay with overhanging pohutukawa dipping into the high tide and the stays gently nudging the mast, sleep comes easily.

Quick Antipasto Picks

For those who cruise the waters for an extended period each summer a well-supplied storecupboard is invaluable. Stock up with deli treats and supplement them with fresh produce for antipasto picks that look impressive but are quickly thrown together. Here are two combinations that work well and look sensational when arranged in clumps over a large white platter and served with sliced Pizza Bread (see page 16).

Finely sliced prosciutto randomly dropped in a pile
Diced or broken pieces of feta cheese
A pile of cherry tomato halves
Marinated green olives
Halved bocconcini
Diced rock melon
Smoked eel, broken into pieces
Handful of rocket leaves
Wedges of limes or lemons

Strips of oven-baked eggplant (see page 20)
Fromage blanc or quark
Yellow and red peppers (capsicums), grilled, skinned and sliced (see page 124)
Pieces of wood-roasted salmon
Kalamata olives
Grilled sliced artichoke halves
Kabayaki dory
Handful of watercress
Wafers of pecorino cheese

Fried Haloumi Cheese with Roasted Garlic and Lemon

This Greek-inspired morsel is a perfect on-deck snack to have with your sundowner.

2 garlic bulbs
olive oil for cooking
250g haloumi cheese
lemon wedges

Cut the garlic bulbs in half horizontally and drizzle a little olive oil on the cut sides. Wrap each garlic half, cut side down, in a square of aluminium foil large enough to seal each package at the top with a twist. Roast the garlic in an oven preheated to 190°C for 30 minutes or until the pulp is tender. Remove from the oven and allow to cool for 20 minutes.

Slice the haloumi cheese and fry with a little oil in a frying pan over a medium–high heat until the haloumi is golden on both sides and squeaks when you bite into it. Stack the haloumi into a random pile on a serving dish and squeeze over the roasted garlic and lemon juice to taste. Eat in your fingers immediately.

SERVES 4–6

Fried haloumi cheese with roasted garlic and lemon

Grilled Herb Mussels

If you are lucky enough to gather mussels on your excursions ashore this is a sizzling way to enjoy the harvest.

36 mussels, scrubbed and bearded
1 cup white wine
2 cups grainy breadcrumbs
$^{1}/_{2}$ cup pine nuts, coarsely chopped
2 tablespoons fresh flat-leaf parsley, finely chopped
3 tablespoons dill, chopped
2 teaspoons grated lemon zest
100g butter, melted
4 tablespoons lemon juice
sea salt and freshly ground black pepper

Place the mussels and wine in a large saucepan over a medium heat and simmer, covered, for 3 minutes or until the mussels open. Drain and discard any unopened shells. Remove the top half of the shells. In a food processor combine the breadcrumbs, pine nuts, parsley, dill, lemon zest, half the butter, half the lemon juice and the seasonings until well mixed. Place the mussels in their shells in an ovenproof dish and spoon the breadcrumb mixture over the mussels. Grill under a medium heat until golden. While the mussels grill, melt together the remaining butter and lemon juice, then drizzle over the cooked mussels hot from the grill.

SERVES 4–6

Grilled herb mussels

Ideas for Oyster Lovers

I acquired a taste for Bluff oysters very early in life. I was lucky to be born and raised in Southland, spitting distance from the Bluff oyster beds. Their abundance frequently led to the total indulgence verging on gluttony. Family culinary dalliances included scalloped oysters, oyster sandwiches (my favourite), oyster cocktail and according to some the ultimate aphrodisiac, whole oysters dropped into a glass of Guinness.

Their short season and price, though slightly prohibitive, hasn't quelled my passion at the thought of that first taste each year. My favourite way to eat any oyster is simply, from the half shell with a squeeze of lemon juice and a grind of freshly ground black pepper. Generally, I prefer my oysters raw, although I can drool over a creamy oyster soup. The other appealing idea is oysters with dipping sauces. Pile your oysters in the shell on a large platter or bowl of ice, and lemon wedges. Supply your diners with forks or skewers and a range of distinctive dipping sauces.

Vinegar Dipping Sauce

1 shallot (eschallot), finely chopped
2 tablespoons sherry vinegar
2 tablespoons red wine vinegar
3 tablespoons balsamic vinegar
a generous amount of freshly ground black pepper

Combine all the ingredients and refrigerate for 1 hour before serving.

MAKES 1/2 CUP

Hot Shot Dipping Sauce

1/2 small red onion, peeled and very finely chopped
1 small stalk celery, very finely chopped
1/4 cup fresh coriander, finely chopped
1/2 cup lemon juice
Tabasco sauce to taste
sea salt and freshly ground black pepper

Combine all the ingredients and refrigerate for 1 hour before serving.

MAKES 1 CUP

Garlic Mayonnaise

1 cup Basic Egg Mayonnaise (see page 78)
2 cloves garlic, crushed

Combine the ingredients.

MAKES 1 CUP

Barbecued Basil Prawns

Although slightly fiddly to prepare, a platter of Basil Prawns served as a pre-dinner snack is always appreciated.

36 large green prawns, shell on
1/2 cup extra virgin olive oil
grated zest of 1 lemon
1/4 cup lemon juice
handful of fresh basil, finely shredded
freshly ground black pepper
lemon for squeezing
2 cups Basic Egg Mayonnaise (see below)

Using a sharp knife, pierce the shells of the prawns and split them open from the back of the head down to the tail and devein. Combine the olive oil, lemon zest and juice and basil, and drizzle over the prawns. Season with pepper. Barbecue the prawns on a medium–high heat for a couple of minutes on each side or until cooked. Squeeze over some lemon juice and serve immediately with Basic Egg Mayonnaise on the side.

SERVES 6

Basic Egg Mayonnaise

4 egg yolks
1 3/4 cups good quality or organic olive oil
4–5 tablespoons lemon juice
sea salt

Place the egg yolks in a food processor. With the motor running add the olive oil drop by drop until mayonnaise thickens. Add a tablespoonful of lemon juice and continue to add the oil in a steady thin drizzle. Add extra lemon juice to taste and adjust the thickness. Season with salt.

If the mayonnaise should separate, don't throw out the curdled mixture: start again with a fresh egg yolk in a clean, dry bowl. Drop by drop, beat in the curdled mixture until the emulsion forms and the mixture has thickened. To stabilise this add a squeeze of lemon juice. Continue adding the curdled mixture in a slow, thin, steady drizzle then add extra oil if you need to.

MAKES 2 CUPS

Barbecued basil prawns

Lemon Battered Fish

A quick, light, crisp batter makes all the difference to whatever you catch on a day out in the dinghy.

500g tarakihi fillets (or any white fish)
1 1/2 cups plain flour
1/2 cup lemon juice
2 teaspoons grated lemon zest
250–300ml soda water
peanut oil for frying

Cut the tarakihi fillets into portions. Sift the flour into a bowl. Gradually stir in the lemon juice, lemon zest and enough soda water to make a thick creamy batter. In a heavy-based saucepan heat to 190°C enough peanut oil for deep-frying. Dip the fish into the batter as you are ready to cook it, allowing the excess batter to drain from the fish. Deep-fry the fish in batches, cooking it for 3–5 minutes depending on the size. The fish should be cooked through and golden.

SERVES 4–6

Crisp Roasted Snapper

If it's snapper you're catching from the boat you'll get an impressive result for little effort when roasting this densely textured fish.

3 teaspoons ground cumin
1 teaspoon smoked paprika
1 fresh red chilli, deseeded
1/4 cup fresh coriander
1/4 cup fresh flat-leaf parsley
2 cloves garlic, peeled
1 teaspoon grated fresh ginger
3 tablespoons olive oil
1 snapper (or any whole white fish), gutted and scaled
olive oil for spraying
freshly ground black pepper
sea salt

Place the cumin, smoked paprika, chilli, coriander, parsley, garlic, ginger and olive oil in a food processor and process to a pulpy paste. Make three or four slits in the flesh of both sides of the fish and smear the spice mixture over it. Cover and marinate in the refrigerator for 1 hour.

Spray the fish on both sides with olive oil spray. Season with salt and pepper. Place in an oiled roasting tin and cook in an oven preheated to 190°C for 20–30 minutes or until crisp and cooked through.

SERVES 6

Canned Sardines and Red Onion Relish on Toast

Sardines, cucumber, toast and relish make a juicy snack for hungry seafarers.

10 slices lightly grilled or barbecued bread
small telegraph cucumber, peeled and sliced
3 x 100g cans sardines in oil
freshly ground black pepper
1 cup Red Onion Relish (see below)

Cover the bread with slices of cucumber, sardines, pepper and a dollop of red onion relish.

SERVES 8

Red Onion Relish

This relish is particularly robust and luscious on snacks and in sandwiches and accompanying grilled meats.

2kg red onions, peeled, halved and finely sliced
100ml olive oil
2 tablespoons grated fresh ginger
1/2 teaspoon ground mixed spice
freshly ground black pepper
3 1/2 cups (packed) brown sugar
1 1/2 cups balsamic vinegar
1 bay leaf

In a heavy-based saucepan cook the onions with the olive oil over a low heat until soft. Add the ginger, mixed spice, pepper, brown sugar, balsamic vinegar and bay leaf and stir until the sugar dissolves. Bring to a gentle boil and simmer for 40 minutes or until thick and syrupy, removing the scum as it appears. Remove the bay leaf. Spoon the onion relish into clean warm jars and seal.

MAKES 6 CUPS

Canned sardines and red onion relish on toast

Clams and Pasta with Parsley Pesto

For this dish you can prepare the clams and pesto before you leave the dock and store them in the boat's refrigerator: all that's left is a little simple cooking and finding a calm bay to sit and enjoy the bold flavours.

2kg southern clams (about 22)
2 cups fresh flat-leaf parsley (packed)
20 baby capers, rinsed
anchovies to taste (I use 2 or 3)
1 clove garlic, peeled
100ml extra virgin olive oil
2–3 tablespoons lemon juice
freshly ground black pepper
400g spaghetti or preferred pasta
salt and olive oil for pasta water
¼ cup white wine

Scrub and soak the clams in water for 30 minutes. While the clams soak make the pesto. Place the parsley, capers, anchovies and garlic in a food processor and pulse to chop the ingredients. With the motor running add the olive oil in a steady stream and process to a smooth paste. Add the lemon juice and pepper to taste.

Place the spaghetti in boiling salted water with a dash of olive oil and simmer until cooked al dente. While the spaghetti is cooking, place the clams and white wine in a saucepan over a medium–high heat and simmer until the clams open. This only takes a couple of minutes once the liquid has boiled.

Drain the spaghetti and tip it into a serving dish, pile on the clams and their juice, spoon over the parsley pesto and gently toss. Alternatively serve the sauce separately.

SERVES 4

Clams and pasta with parsley pesto

Prawn Rolls with Cocktail Sauce

If you're out doing some serious sailing you'll find this hand-held lunch convenient and refreshing.

½ cup sour cream
grated zest of 1 lemon
2 tablespoons lemon juice
1 clove garlic, peeled and finely chopped
1 fresh red chilli, deseeded and finely chopped
2 tablespoons fresh coriander, chopped
500g green prawns, peeled and deveined
olive oil for frying
8 crusty rolls (or French sticks cut into chunks)
2 cups mesclun leaves
1¼ cups Cocktail Sauce (see below)

Combine the sour cream, lemon zest and juice, garlic, chilli and coriander in a bowl. Add the prawns and stir thoroughly to coat. Marinate, covered, for 30 minutes in the refrigerator. Grill the prawns in batches with a little olive oil for 3–4 minutes on each side or until the prawns are cooked through. Split the rolls or French bread and fill with prawns, mesclun leaves and a generous dollop of Cocktail Sauce.

SERVES 8

Cocktail Sauce

150ml cream, whipped
150ml good quality store-bought organic tomato sauce
1 teaspoon Worcestershire sauce
1 tablespoon lemon juice
1 tablespoon sweet chilli sauce
sea salt

Place all the ingredients in a bowl and fold together until combined.

MAKES 1½ CUPS

Coconut and Lemon Risotto Cakes with Walnut Mayonnaise and Crayfish

For a special meal at the beach, arborio rice flavoured with coconut and lemon provides a satisfying platform for the delicate taste of crayfish.

1 onion, peeled and finely chopped
2 cloves garlic, peeled and finely chopped
2 tablespoons olive oil
2 cups arborio rice
4 cups chicken stock, warmed
$^1/_2$ cup coconut cream
grated zest of 1 lemon
$^1/_4$ cup grated parmesan cheese
1 cup fresh breadcrumbs
1 teaspoon lemon juice
2 eggs
salt and freshly ground black pepper
olive oil for frying
1$^1/_2$ cups Walnut Mayonnaise (see below)
2 cooked shelled crayfish tails, sliced into 5mm pieces

Gently sauté the onion and garlic in the olive oil until soft. Stir in the arborio rice and gently cook for 2 minutes. Raise the heat to medium–high and begin to add the warmed chicken stock a little at a time. Stir the rice as it cooks and absorbs the stock before adding more. Add the stock as required until the rice is tender. Stir in coconut cream, lemon zest and parmesan cheese, and allow to cool.

Combine the risotto and breadcrumbs in a bowl. Add the lemon juice and eggs, mix together well and season to taste. The mixture should be sticky enough to hold together when rolled into a ball and flattened. If it is too sloppy, add some more breadcrumbs. With wet hands form the mixture into eight 10cm cakes approximately 1cm thick. Refrigerate for 15 minutes before cooking. Shallow fry the cakes in batches in hot oil until golden and crisp on both sides. Drain on kitchen paper.

Finish the top of each cake with a dollop of Walnut Mayonnaise and a couple of slices of crayfish.

SERVES 4–6

Walnut Mayonnaise

2 egg yolks
grated zest of 1 lemon
1 cup extra virgin olive oil
4 tablespoons walnut oil
4 tablespoons lemon juice
sea salt

Place the egg yolks and lemon zest in a food processor. Drop by drop add the olive oil until it thickens. Continue to add the olive oil then walnut oil in a steady, thin stream until thick. Add the lemon juice to thin and salt to taste.

MAKES 1$^1/_2$ CUPS

Coconut and lemon risotto cakes with walnut mayonnaise and crayfish

Fresh Summer Salad with Pesto Dressing

Tomatoes, cucumbers and avocados are summer staples. With salad greens, feta cheese and some pesto on hand you can create this crunchy salad in a flash.

1 telegraph cucumber, peeled
2 cups cherry tomatoes
2 large tomatoes, coarsely chopped
1 large firm avocado, peeled, stoned and chopped into large chunks
150g cows milk feta cheese broken into large pieces
1/2 cup Pesto Dressing (see below)
1–2 cups rocket leaves or salad greens

Cut the cucumber in half lengthways, remove the core and cut into large chunks. Place the cucumber, cherry and chopped tomatoes, avocado and feta in a serving bowl. Just before serving, drizzle the salad with Pesto Dressing and toss gently. Either toss the salad greens through the salad or simply pile on top of the salad.

SERVES 6

Pesto Dressing

1/4 cup extra virgin olive oil
2 tablespoons lemon juice
2 tablespoons store-bought basil pesto
sea salt

Shake all the ingredients together and gently toss with the salad.

MAKES 1/2 CUP

Fresh summer salad with pesto dressing

Peanut Chicken with Pawpaw and Avocado Salsa

How about a tantalising chicken breast with a spicy textured top and soft juicy salsa?

$1\frac{1}{2}$ cups roasted unsalted peanuts
$\frac{1}{4}$ cup red Thai curry paste
$\frac{1}{2}$ cup fresh coriander
$\frac{1}{2}$ cup fresh basil
$\frac{1}{2}$ cup coconut cream
6 single chicken breasts (tenderloin removed)
3 cups Pawpaw and Avocado Salsa (see below)

Place the peanuts, curry paste, coriander, basil and coconut cream in a food processor and pulse until just combined and the nuts are coarsely chopped.

Place the chicken breasts in an oiled ovenproof dish. Divide the peanut mixture between the breasts, spreading it evenly on top. Bake in a preheated oven (at 190°C), uncovered, for 20 minutes or until the topping is golden and the chicken juices run clear when a skewer is inserted. Allow to rest for 10 minutes before slicing into thick pieces and serving with Pawpaw and Avocado Salsa.

SERVES 6

Pawpaw and Avocado Salsa

1 firm ripe pawpaw
2 firm ripe avocados
1 red onion, peeled and finely chopped
1 cup fresh mint, finely shredded

DRESSING

2 tablespoons extra virgin olive oil
1 tablespoon lime juice
1 tablespoon red wine vinegar
sea salt

Halve, seed, quarter and peel the pawpaw. Peel and stone the avocado. Finely dice the pawpaw and avocado and place in a bowl with the red onion and mint. Mix all the dressing ingredients together and drizzle it over the salsa.

MAKES 3 CUPS

Salmon Kedgeree

Make a satisfying and sustaining breakfast, lunch or brunch dish from easily available storecupboard ingredients.

4 1/2 cups water for rice
1 1/2 cups basmati rice
1 1/2 teaspoons ground turmeric
1 bay leaf
4 tablespoons butter
3 onions, peeled and sliced
200g wood-roasted salmon, broken into pieces
1/2 cup fresh flat-leaf parsley, chopped
sea salt and freshly ground black pepper
pinch of smoked paprika
4 hard-boiled eggs, peeled and quartered
2 tablespoons butter
8 poppadoms

Boil the water in a large saucepan, add the rice, turmeric and bay leaf, and cook for 15 minutes or until tender. Drain the rice and discard the bay leaf. Keep the rice warm. Melt the first measure of butter in a frying pan and fry the onions until brown. Drain on absorbent kitchen paper. Add the rice to the pan, then half the onions, the salmon, parsley, seasonings, paprika, eggs and second measure of butter. Reheat, stirring gently, and spoon into a serving dish. Sprinkle the remaining onions on top and serve with poppadoms.

SERVES 4

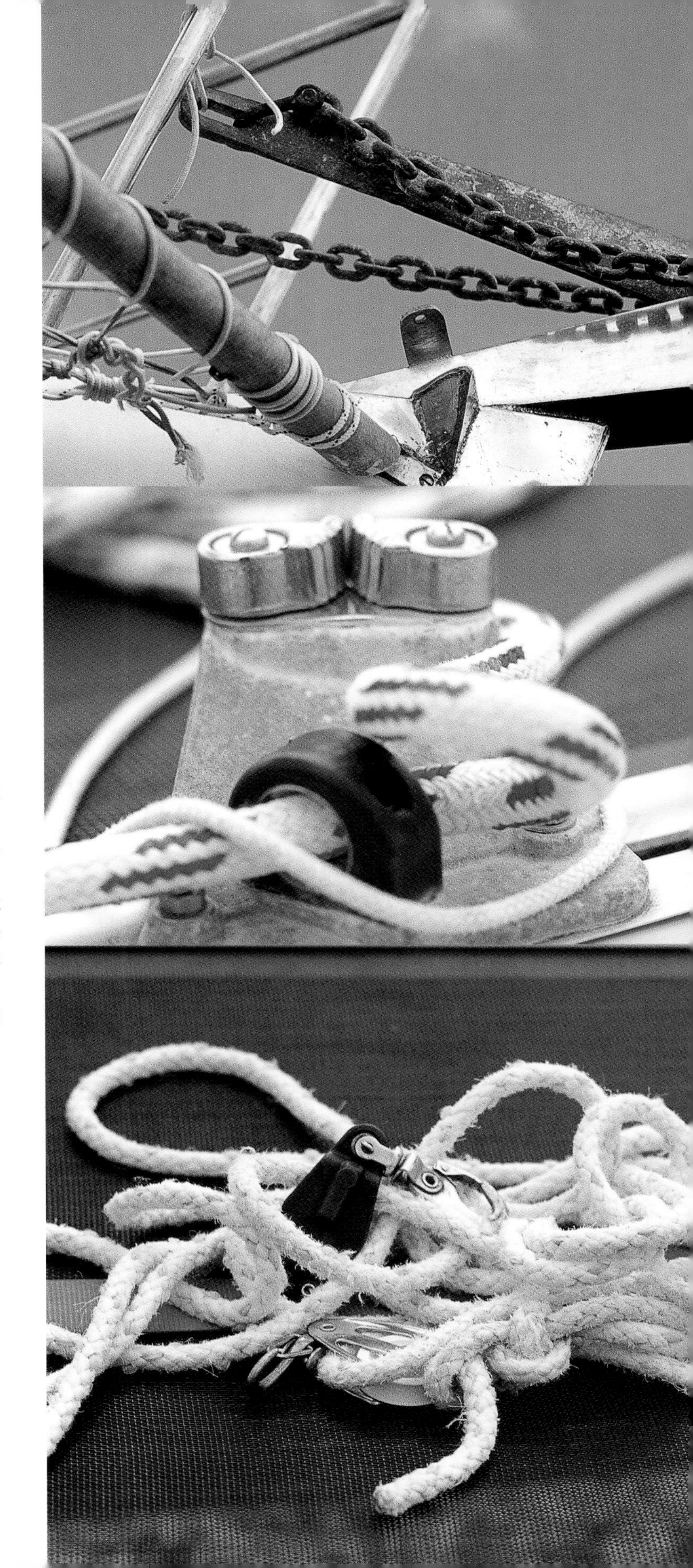

Meatballs and Couscous with Cumberland Sauce

This marriage of Middle Eastern and traditional English flavours is slightly more challenging to make but well worth the effort. Make them well in advance and freeze for convenience.

MEATBALLS

400g minced lean beef or veal
400g minced lean lamb
1 red onion, peeled and very finely chopped
3 cloves garlic, peeled and crushed
2 teaspoons dukkah
2 slices white bread, crusts removed, soaked in milk and squeezed dry
1 teaspoon grated lemon zest
1/4 cup sesame seeds, toasted
1/2 cup fresh flat-leaf parsley, finely chopped
1/2 cup fresh mint, finely chopped
2 small eggs
sea salt and freshly ground black pepper
plain flour for dusting
oil for cooking

COUSCOUS

250ml water
250ml chicken stock
1/2 teaspoon salt
1 tablespoon olive oil
2 cups couscous
3 tablespoons butter
grated zest of 1 lemon
grated zest of 1 orange
squeeze of lemon juice
squeeze of orange juice
1/4 cup sultanas
1/4 cup pistachio nuts, shelled
1/4 cup fresh flat-leaf parsley, finely chopped
sea salt and freshly ground black pepper

2 cups Cumberland Sauce (see opposite)

To make the meatballs, mix the ingredients together well. Roll into small meatballs and lightly dust with flour. Using a little oil to prevent sticking bake the meatballs in a roasting pan in an oven preheated to 180°C for 15–20 minutes or until brown and slightly crisp. Drain on absorbent kitchen paper.

To make the couscous, place the water, chicken stock, salt and olive oil in a saucepan and bring to the boil. Remove from the heat and stir in the couscous. Cover and allow the grains to swell and absorb the liquid for 2–3 minutes. Stir the butter through to separate the grains, add the grated zest, juice, sultanas, pistachios, parsley and seasonings.

Heap the couscous onto a serving platter and pile the meatballs alongside. Serve the warm sauce on the side.

SERVES 8

Cumberland Sauce

2 shallots (eschallots), finely chopped
zest of 2 oranges
1/4 cup water
1/2 cup orange juice
1/2 cup lemon juice
1 tablespoon caster sugar
1 teaspoon hot English mustard mixed to a paste with balsamic vinegar
1/2 teaspoon grated fresh ginger
2/3 cup redcurrant jelly
1/3 cup port

Simmer the shallots and orange zest together in the water for 5 minutes and drain. Add the remaining ingredients, mix together and gently simmer over a low heat for 10–15 minutes. Allow to cool a little.

MAKES 2 CUPS

Raw Fish Salad

This clean, refreshing dish is very quick to make.

1kg filleted white fish (snapper, tarakihi, hapuku)
1 cup lime or lemon juice
1/2 cup coconut cream
1/2 red pepper (capsicum), halved and deseeded
1/2 yellow pepper (capsicum), halved and deseeded
2 firm ripe avocados, peeled and stoned
2 small red onions, peeled, halved and finely sliced
1 cup (loosely packed) fresh coriander
1/4 cup chives, finely sliced
1 fresh red chilli, deseeded and finely chopped
3 tablespoons coconut cream
freshly ground black pepper

Slice the fish into bite-sized pieces and place in a bowl that holds it snugly. Pour the lemon or lime juice and first measure of coconut cream over and coat the fish well. Cover and refrigerate for at least 45 minutes or until the fish whitens. Finely chop the red and yellow peppers and roughly dice the avocados. Place the peppers and avocados on a serving platter. Add the sliced onions, coriander, chives and chilli. Strain half the marinade from the fish and pile fish onto the salad. Spoon the second measure of coconut cream over and season with pepper. Toss gently and serve.

SERVES 6–8

Raw fish salad

GLENDARA
WOOD

Lamb Terrine

Tasty and quick to make, this dish is perfect with fresh French or rustic country bread and a savoury jam or relish such as Beetroot and Apple Relish (see page 42).

1 large red onion, peeled and finely chopped
3 cloves garlic, peeled and finely chopped
125g pancetta or bacon, finely chopped
2 tablespoons olive oil
1/4 cup sweet chilli sauce
1/4 cup sun-dried tomato paste
2 tablespoons Worcestershire sauce
1/2 cup fresh breadcrumbs
freshly ground black pepper
1.25kg lean minced lamb
1 egg
8–10 thin slices streaky bacon

Fry the onion, garlic and pancetta in the olive oil over a medium heat until the onion is soft. Transfer to a bowl and add the sweet chilli sauce, sun-dried tomato paste, Worcestershire sauce, breadcrumbs, pepper, minced lamb and egg. Combine well. Line two 5-cup capacity loaf tins with streaky bacon, placing the bacon across the tin and allowing the ends to hang over the edge. Put the meat mixture in the tin or tins and fold over the bacon ends. Bake in an oven preheated to 200°C for 45 minutes to 1 hour. Serve hot or cold.

SERVES 8–10

Chocolate Nut Bars

Easy and indulgent.

500g good quality dark cooking chocolate
400g can sweetened condensed milk
1/2 cup nuts (almonds, walnuts, hazelnuts, brazil, pistachio nuts)
Dutch cocoa powder

Gently melt the chocolate and condensed milk together over a low heat. Add the nuts and stir to combine. Pour the mixture into a lightly greased 20cm x 20cm baking tin and spread evenly. Refrigerate for 1 hour.

Cut into small bars and roll in the cocoa powder.

MAKES 40

Caramel, Lemon and Pistachio Fudge

This is a guaranteed winner for those with a sweet tooth. Serve it with coffee and store in an airtight container in the refrigerator.

397g can caramel condensed milk
375g Vanilla Wine Biscuits (plain sweet biscuits), coarsely crushed
75g butter, melted
1 cup pistachio nuts, coarsely chopped
grated zest of 1 lemon
2 tablespoons lemon juice
1/4 cup pistachio nuts, chopped

ICING

2 1/2 cups icing sugar, sifted
grated zest of 1 lemon
2–3 tablespoons lemon juice
50g butter, melted
1 tablespoon water

Combine the condensed milk, biscuit crumbs, butter, first measure of pistachios, and lemon zest and juice. Press into a 28cm x 28cm baking tin and chill.

To make the icing, combine the icing sugar, lemon zest and juice, butter and water in a bowl and beat until smooth. Spread evenly over the base and sprinkle the second measure of pistachios on top. Chill until the topping is set.

Cut into thin bars.

MAKES 40

Chocolate Coffee-bean Biscotti

Stored in an airtight container biscotti will last for ages, so they're ideal for after-dinner treats if you're cruising the briny for a couple of weeks.

2 1/4 cups plain flour
1 1/2 teaspoons baking powder
60g butter, cubed
1 cup caster sugar
1 cup ground almonds
1/4 cup chocolate-covered coffee beans, coarsely chopped
3 small eggs, lightly beaten
cocoa powder for dusting

Sift the flour and baking powder together. Rub the butter in until the mixture resembles fine breadcrumbs. Stir in the caster sugar, almonds and coffee beans. Make a well in the centre, add the eggs and mix to a firm dough.

Knead the dough on a floured surface until it looks smooth. Divide the dough in half. Roll out each half into 5cm-wide logs and flatten slightly. Place on a greased tray and lightly dust with cocoa powder. Bake the logs in an oven preheated to 180°C for 40 minutes or until cooked through. Remove from the oven and allow to stand for 15 minutes. Cut diagonally into 1cm slices and lay on an oven tray. Bake at 180°C for 5 minutes on each side or until lightly golden. Allow to cool.

MAKES 30–40

barbecue

At the first hint of summer warmth in the rays of the sun, they are dragged from their caves like grouchy hibernating bears in spring. Stainless steel, state-of-the-art, gas-fired marvel or hinged sausage sizzler over hot coals, they are poked and prodded into life, the cobwebs dusted and the rust scraped off – the barbie is fired up and the ritual begins.

Barbecuing is in our blood. The earliest form of cooking, it has been around for half a million years, ever since our ancestors first created a hearth and dropped food directly onto the embers of the fire. Before too long they would construct barbecue grills from stones, spit-roast meat by putting small pieces on sticks and holding them over the fire, and stew food by wrapping it in leaves and placing it in the ashes to cook. Cooking over an open fire remains a favourite way to cook, with modern barbecuing being invented (and the term adopted) in the southern states of America in the eighteenth century.

Through howling winds, summer cyclones, unbearable heat and empty gas bottles we Kiwis will barbecue anywhere – at home, at the beach or park or on a boat. A meal of seared sausages and steak sandwiches cooked by Dad accompanied with boiled potatoes and salads prepared by Mum is the essence of the traditional New Zealand summer. And yet barbecue cooking has the potential to be so much more than charred remains and coleslaw: fresh meat, fish and vegetables sealed on a sizzling hot grill can be tasty, exotic and flavour infused. With a little imagination barbecue season, always a time for easy gatherings of family and friends, can also be a delight for the taste buds.

Barbecued Crayfish Tails

Use crayfish or lobster for this melt-in-the-mouth grown-up treat. It is a wonderful starter served as is or with Basic Egg Mayonnaise (see page 78) and a crisp green salad.

1 1/4 cups fresh basil, coarsely chopped
1 clove garlic, peeled and crushed
grated zest of 1 lemon
2 tablespoons lemon juice
1 teaspoon dukkah
1/2 cup olive oil
sea salt and freshly ground black pepper
3 uncooked crayfish tails

To make the marinade, place the basil, garlic, lemon zest and juice, and dukkah in a food processor and reduce to a paste. Slowly add the olive oil while continuing to process. Season to taste. Refrigerate until ready to use.

Halve the crayfish tails lengthways and generously baste with the marinade. Grill shell side down on an oiled barbecue over a medium–high heat. Baste the flesh generously with the dressing while it cooks. Allow 10–12 minutes on each side.

SERVES 6

Barbecued Scallops with Coriander and Lime Chilli Butter

36 southern scallops on the half shell
50g butter, softened
1 cup fresh coriander, finely shredded
grated zest of 1 lime
2 teaspoons lime juice
1 fresh red chilli, deseeded and finely chopped
1 clove garlic, peeled and crushed

If you cannot find scallops on the half shell, remove the top shell, lift out the scallop and clean. Return the scallops to their half shells. Mix the butter, coriander, lime zest and juice, chilli and garlic to a paste. Place 1/2 teaspoon coriander butter in each scallop shell. Place the shells on a barbecue over a medium–high heat and cook for 2–3 minutes or until the scallops just turn white. Serve straight from the barbecue.

SERVES 6

Barbecued scallops with coriander
and lime chilli butter

Hapuku Fillets with Chermoula Sauce

A quick whizz in the food processor and you have a spicy Middle Eastern sauce to spike up barbecued fish.

800g fresh hapuku fillets (or other white fish fillets)
3 tablespoons olive oil
1 1/4 cups Chermoula Sauce (see below)
1 tablespoon grated lemon zest

Brush the fish with a little olive oil and Chermoula Sauce. Sprinkle the lemon zest over. Place on an oiled barbecue plate and cook over a high heat for 3–4 minutes on each side or until the flesh is cooked through. Serve with Chermoula Sauce on the side.

SERVES 6

Chermoula Sauce

1 cup fresh flat-leaf parsley
1 cup fresh coriander
1/2 cup fresh mint
2 cloves garlic, peeled
1 teaspoon ground cumin
2 small fresh red chillies, deseeded and chopped
1/4 cup lemon juice
1/2 teaspoon sweet ground paprika
1/2 teaspoon ground turmeric
1/2 cup extra virgin olive oil
sea salt

Place all the ingredients in a food processor and blend to a smooth paste. Taste and adjust the seasonings to suit your palate. If you prefer a thinner sauce add extra oil.

MAKES 1 1/4 CUPS

Hapuku fillets with chermoula sauce

Lemon Honey Chicken with Honey Mustard Mayonnaise

With its sweet-sour flavours, this tasty barbecued chicken dish is an easy meal to make for friends.

6 single chicken breasts, skin removed
2 tablespoons honey
2 cloves garlic, peeled and crushed
1 fresh red chilli, deseeded and finely chopped
1/4 cup lemon juice
2 tablespoons soy sauce
2 tablespoons olive oil
3 tablespoons balsamic vinegar
freshly ground black pepper
1 cup Honey Mustard Mayonnaise (see below)
watercress for serving

Trim the chicken breasts and shallow score each side in a criss-cross pattern. Make a marinade by combining the honey, garlic, chilli, lemon juice, soy sauce, olive oil, balsamic vinegar and pepper. Place the chicken breasts in the marinade, cover and leave for 2 hours in the refrigerator.

Place the chicken breasts on an oiled barbecue grill over a medium–high heat, basting occasionally with the marinade. Barbecue for 5 minutes on each side or until the juices run clear when a skewer is inserted.

Serve the chicken breasts whole or sliced and stacked with a splodge of Honey Mustard Mayonnaise and watercress on the side.

SERVES 6

Honey Mustard Mayonnaise

2 egg yolks
1/2 tablespoon mild mustard
sea salt and freshly ground black pepper
125–150ml extra virgin olive oil
3–4 tablespoons lemon juice
1/4 cup honey
2 tablespoons sherry vinegar
1/4 cup fresh basil, finely shredded

Place the egg yolks, mustard, salt and pepper in a food processor. With the motor running add the olive oil drop by drop until the mayonnaise thickens. Continue to add the oil in a thin steady drizzle. Add lemon juice, honey and sherry vinegar to taste. Lastly add the basil and stir in. Leave to stand for 1 hour before serving to allow the basil to infuse the mayonnaise.

MAKES 1 CUP

Ginger Pork and Kumara Salad

Ginger up barbecued pork with this quick, simple marinade and salad.

8 pork scotch fillets, trimmed
3 tablespoons grated fresh ginger
4 tablespoons soy sauce
freshly ground black pepper

SALAD
800g golden kumara, peeled
3 tablespoons olive oil
1/2 teaspoon smoked paprika
sea salt and freshly ground black pepper
2 tablespoons lemon juice
1/3 cup sweet chilli sauce
1 tablespoon extra virgin olive oil

Place the pork in a shallow dish with the ginger, soy sauce and pepper. Coat well with the marinade and leave in the refrigerator for 30 minutes.

To make the salad, cut the kumara into wedges and place in a baking dish. Drizzle the olive oil over and season with smoked paprika, salt and pepper. Bake in a roasting pan in an oven preheated to 180°C for 30 minutes or until soft and browned. Remove from the pan. Shake together the lemon juice, sweet chilli sauce and olive oil and drizzle over the kumara.

Barbecue the steaks on a lightly oiled grill over a high heat for 3–4 minutes on each side or until cooked to your liking. Serve with a dollop of Avocado and Mango Salsa (see page 120) and Kumara Salad on the side.

SERVES 8

Ginger pork and kumara salad, with avocado and mango salsa

Barbecued balsamic steaks, with Stewart's salty sautéed spuds, and chargrilled asparagus

Barbecued Balsamic Steaks

This tender steak is wonderful served with crisp sautéed spuds and chargrilled asparagus. The balsamic vinegar gives it a real flavour blast.

4 tablespoons olive oil
1 cup balsamic vinegar
cracked pepper
6 x 3cm-thick beef steaks

To make the marinade, combine the olive oil, balsamic vinegar and cracked pepper in a shallow dish just big enough to contain the steaks. Leave the steaks in the marinade for at least 10 minutes. Cook the steaks on a hot grill for 4–5 minutes on each side to sear and seal in the juice, basting with the marinade occasionally.

SERVES 6

Burgers with Eggplant Pickle and Yoghurt Sauce

This sophisticated burger is spiced with a sharp pickle and softened with yoghurt sauce.

600g minced lean lamb or beef
1 onion, peeled and finely chopped
2 cloves garlic, peeled and crushed
1 teaspoon ground cumin
1 teaspoon ground coriander
1 banana, mashed
1 tablespoon sweet chilli sauce
2 tablespoons soy sauce
1/2 cup fresh breadcrumbs
2 tablespoons toasted sesame seeds
sea salt and freshly ground black pepper
8 slices of a favourite grainy bread or roll, oiled and lightly grilled
1 1/2 cups Yoghurt Sauce (see opposite)
Eggplant Pickle (see opposite) for serving
2 cups crisp salad greens

Combine the lamb or beef, onion, garlic, spices, banana, sweet chilli sauce, soy sauce, breadcrumbs, sesame seeds, salt and pepper. Shape into eight meat patties. Grill on an oiled barbecue over a medium heat for 8–10 minutes on each side. Assemble the burger by spreading the grilled bread with a little Yoghurt Sauce. Top with the burger, Eggplant Pickle to taste and a little more Yoghurt Sauce. Finish with a handful of salad greens.

SERVES 8

Yoghurt Sauce

500ml plain acidophilus yoghurt
2 cloves garlic, peeled and crushed
1/2 telegraph cucumber, peeled, cored and finely chopped
1 tablespoon fresh mint, finely chopped

To make yoghurt cheese, line a wire sieve with damp absorbent kitchen paper and pour the yoghurt in. Allow it to drain for 1 hour to form a thick paste. Stir the garlic, cucumber and mint through the yoghurt cheese.

MAKES 1 1/2 CUPS

Eggplant Pickle

1 large eggplant (aubergine)
1 onion, peeled and finely chopped
3 cloves garlic, peeled and crushed
1/4 cup olive oil
1 tablespoon grated fresh ginger
1/2 teaspoon ground turmeric
1 tablespoon hot chilli sauce
400g can tomatoes in juice, chopped
1 cup brown sugar
1/4 cup balsamic vinegar
3/4 cup water
sea salt and freshly ground black pepper

Trim the eggplant and dice into small pieces. Shallow fry the onion and garlic in the olive oil over a medium heat until soft. Add the eggplant and brown and soften for 5 minutes. Add the ginger, turmeric, chilli sauce, tomatoes, brown sugar, vinegar and water, and season with salt and pepper. Simmer for 30 minutes or until soft and thick. Spoon into warm clean jars and seal, and store in a cool dark place. Refrigerate for up to six weeks after opening. This pickle is a great cupboard filler to have on hand to accompany grilled and cold meats.

MAKES 4 CUPS

Skewered Spiced Lamb and Sweet Onions

This succulent dish is delicious on rice, tossed with grated lemon zest and pistachio nuts. Alternatively, remove the meat from the skewers and wrap it up in unleavened flat bread with the sweet onions, salad greens and rice – and eat it in your hands.

3 large onions, peeled and finely sliced
2 cloves garlic, peeled and finely chopped
3 tablespoons vegetable oil
2 teaspoons ground coriander
1 tablespoon Thai-style red curry paste
1 teaspoon hot chilli sauce
sea salt and freshly ground black pepper
2 tablespoons apricot jam
2 tablespoons brown sugar
1/2 cup lemon or lime juice
1/2 cup water
800g lamb rump, trimmed and cubed

To make the marinade, fry the onions and garlic in the oil over a low heat until soft. Add the coriander, red curry paste, chilli sauce, salt, pepper, apricot jam and brown sugar and cook for 2 minutes. Stir in the lemon or lime juice and water and simmer gently for 15 minutes. Allow to cool. Mix the cubed lamb into the marinade and leave in the refrigerator for 2 hours, stirring occasionally.

Thread the meat onto metal skewers or wooden skewers soaked in water. Reserve the marinade and onion. Cook the lamb on an oiled barbecue grill over a medium–high heat for 5 minutes each side. Cook the marinade and onions on the barbecue plate until soft and caramelised. Randomly stack the lamb skewers on a serving dish and spoon the onions over.

SERVES 6–8

Sticky Pork Ribs

These sweet, sticky spareribs are definitely a hands-on experience.

2kg (about 4 racks) pork spareribs, cut
6 tablespoons soy sauce
6 tablespoons tomato sauce (ketchup)
1/4 cup lemon juice
3 tablespoons brown sugar
3 tablespoons liquid honey
3 tablespoons sweet sherry
3 tablespoons hoisin sauce
3 cloves garlic, peeled and crushed
2 tablespoons olive oil

In a shallow dish just large enough to hold the ribs marinate the spareribs in all the remaining ingredients mixed together. Thoroughly coat the ribs with the marinade, cover and refrigerate for at least 3 hours (preferably overnight), turning the ribs occasionally.

Place the marinated ribs on an oiled barbecue grill over a medium heat. Grill, basting occasionally with the marinade, for 7–10 minutes each side or until the meat is opaque, golden and still juicy. Pile the ribs onto a serving plate and hand out the paper napkins.

SERVES 6–8

Coconut Pork Satay with Roasted Peanut Sauce

MARINADE

2 shallots (eschallots), chopped roughly
2 cloves garlic, peeled
1 large fresh red chilli, deseeded
1 tablespoon grated fresh ginger
1 tablespoon lime juice
1 tablespoon soy sauce
1 tablespoon grated palm sugar
1 teaspoon ground coriander
freshly ground black pepper
3 tablespoons coconut cream

500g pork scotch fillet cut into 4cm cubes
1 $^{1}/_{2}$ cups Roasted Peanut Sauce (see below)
lemon wedges to garnish
sprigs of fresh coriander to garnish

To make the marinade, place all the ingredients in a food processor and blend to a paste. Combine the pork pieces and paste and thoroughly coat the meat. Cover and refrigerate for 2 hours. Thread the pork onto skewers and grill over a medium–high heat for 10 minutes or until cooked through, golden but still juicy. Randomly stack the skewered pork on a serving platter and garnish with lemon wedges and coriander. Serve with Roasted Peanut Sauce.

SERVES 6

Roasted Peanut Sauce

1 tablespoon peanut oil
1 clove garlic, peeled and crushed
1 shallot (eschallot), finely chopped
2 fresh red chillies, deseeded and finely chopped
250g unsalted peanuts, roasted and coarsely ground
1 tablespoon brown sugar
squeeze of lemon juice
250ml coconut cream
$^{1}/_{4}$ cup smooth peanut butter
sea salt

Heat the oil in a frying pan over a medium heat and fry the garlic, shallot and chillies until soft and golden. Add the peanuts, brown sugar, lemon juice, coconut milk and peanut butter. Gently simmer until thickened. Season with salt.

MAKES 1 $^{1}/_{2}$ CUPS

Avocado and Mango Salsa

2 mangos, peeled and diced
2 firm, ripe avocados, peeled, stoned and diced
1 red onion, peeled, halved and finely chopped
1/4 cup fresh mint, shredded
1/4 cup fresh basil, shredded

DRESSING
1/4 cup extra virgin olive oil
2 cloves garlic, peeled and crushed
1 fresh red chilli, deseeded and finely chopped
2 tablespoons lemon juice
sea salt
dash of Tabasco sauce

Gently combine the mangos, avocados, red onion, mint and basil in a mixing bowl. In a separate bowl combine all the ingredients for the dressing, then drizzle it over the salad and gently stir through at least 30 minutes before serving to allow the flavours to develop.

SERVES 6–8

Richard Hill Oliver's Tomato, Cheese and Onion Pie

A good quality tasty cheddar is the key ingredient in this vegetarian pie, which is uncommonly tasty and moreish served with barbecued lamb and beef. It's a great recipe for those times when there seems to be nothing around.

2 onions, peeled, halved and finely sliced
freshly ground black pepper
6 tomatoes, sliced
50g butter, cut into small cubes
250g tasty cheddar cheese, grated
2 slices stale white bread
2 tablespoons fresh flat-leaf parsley
2 tablespoons fresh sage
sea salt and freshly ground black pepper

Place half the onion slices in a layer in the bottom of a greased 6–8-cup capacity pie dish and season with pepper. Follow with half the tomatoes. Dot the tomatoes with one-third of the cubed butter. Spread half the cheese over. Repeat this process and press the layers firmly down with your hand. Process the bread, parsley and sage together in a blender or food processor to a fine crumb. Sprinkle the breadcrumbs evenly over the top of the pie and dot with the remaining third of butter. Season the top with salt and pepper. Bake in an oven preheated to 170°C for 1 hour.

SERVES 6

Barbecued Butterflied Leg of Lamb

A barbecued leg of lamb is a great way of feeding a crowd, but cooking a large lump of meat is a daunting prospect. To make preparation easy, ask your butcher to bone and butterfly your lamb leg and follow this fail-safe step-by-step method. Use your favourite marinade or paste or stud your meat with garlic, fresh rosemary, or thyme sprigs.

1. Trim the excess fat from a 1.5kg butterflied leg of lamb.
2. Lay the lamb on a flat surface.
3. Score both sides of the meat in a criss–cross pattern with a sharp knife.
4. Marinate the meat with your favourite marinade, or stud it with garlic, fresh rosemary or thyme sprigs.
5. Weave two metal skewers through the length of the meat to allow easy turning.
6. Place the lamb on a lightly oiled barbecue grill over a medium–high heat.
7. Grill for about 20 minutes on each side for a medium–rare result.
8. To retain the juices and make carving easier, allow the meat to stand for 15 minutes before slicing.

SERVES 6–8

Barbecued butterflied leg of lamb

Chargrilled New Potatoes with Roasted Red Pepper Mayonnaise

1kg unpeeled small new season's potatoes
3 cloves garlic, peeled and crushed
$^1/_4$ cup olive oil
freshly ground black pepper
1$^1/_2$ cups Roasted Red Pepper Mayonnaise (see below)

Boil the potatoes for approximately 10 minutes or until just tender. Drain and run under cold water to cool. Dry the potatoes and cut any large potatoes in half. Combine the garlic, olive oil and seasonings in a bowl. Toss the potatoes in the oil until well coated. Cook the potatoes on an oiled barbecue grill over a medium heat, turning regularly. Cook until they are lightly charred and crisp. Serve hot with Roasted Red Pepper Mayonnaise.

SERVES 6

Roasted Red Pepper Mayonnaise

2 egg yolks
1 teaspoon Dijon mustard
2 cloves garlic, peeled and crushed
1 cup extra virgin olive oil
1 red pepper (capsicum), deseeded, roasted, skinned, and sliced
$^1/_2$ teaspoon ground paprika
1–2 tablespoons lemon juice
sea salt

Place the egg yolks, mustard and garlic in a food processor. With the motor running add the olive oil drop by drop until the mayonnaise thickens. Continue to add the oil in a steady thin drizzle until finished. Add the red pepper, paprika, lemon juice and salt to taste. Process to a smooth mayonnaise.

MAKES 1$^1/_2$ CUPS

Roasting and Skinning Peppers

Use an electric grill or the oven. Halve the peppers and remove the seeds and white ribs. Oil the peppers, place them cut side down on aluminium foil on a baking tray and grill or roast in a hot oven until the skin blackens. Place the peppers in a plastic bag or cover with a cloth for 15 minutes then, when they are cool enough to handle, peel off the skins.

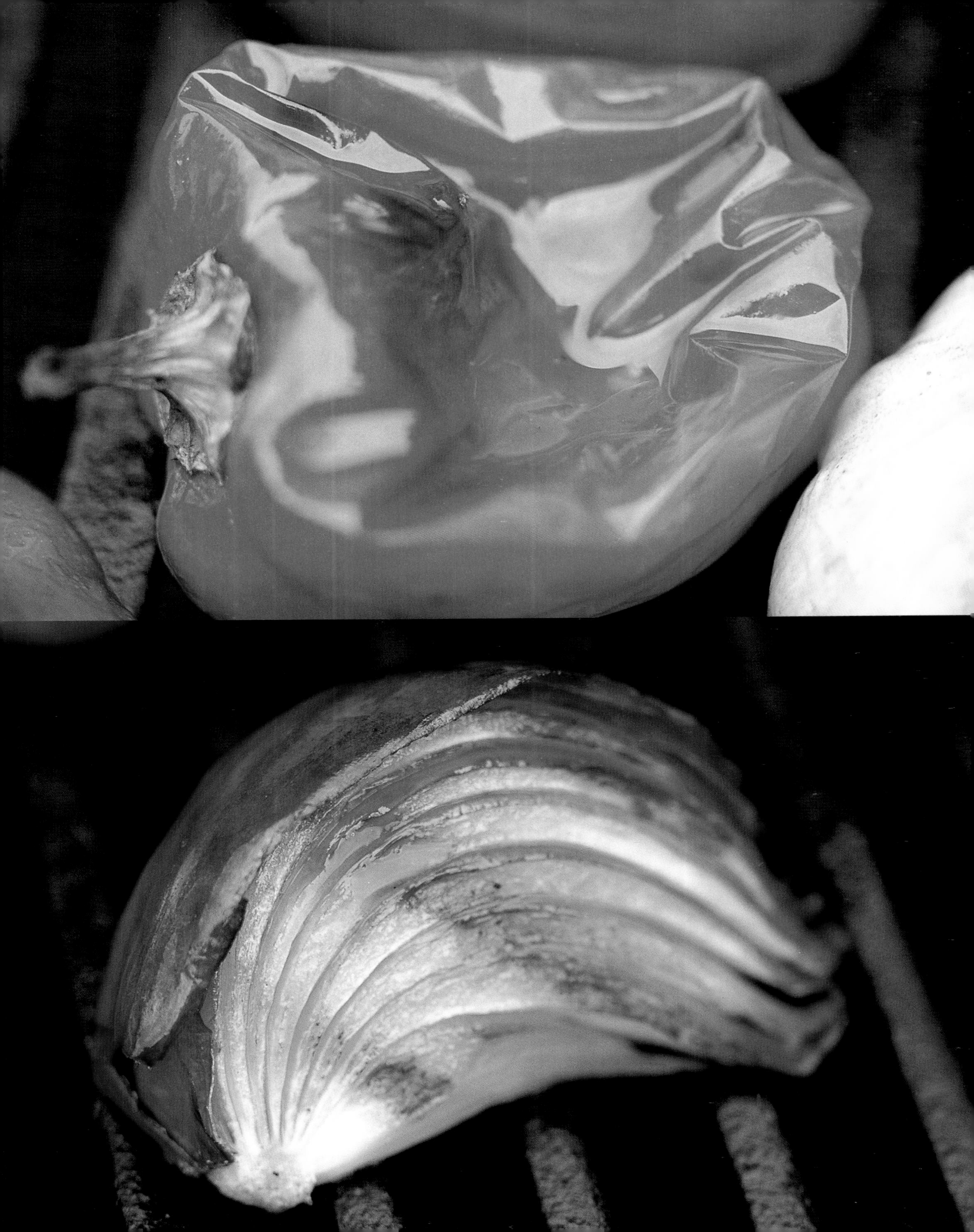

Chargrilled Asparagus with Basil Dressing

Nutty barbecued asparagus and fresh basil epitomise the taste of summer.

600g fresh asparagus
olive oil for brushing or spraying
sea salt
3/4 cup Basil Dressing (see below)

Snap the ends from the asparagus spears and blanch in boiling water for about 10 seconds, until they turn bright green. Drain and run under cold water for 2 minutes. Thoroughly dry. Brush or spray with olive oil and season with salt. Grill over a medium–hot barbecue until they are slightly charred but still crunchy. Lay on a serving platter and drizzle the Basil Dressing over or serve it on the side.

SERVES 6–8

Basil Dressing

1 1/2 cups fresh basil, coarsely chopped
1 clove garlic, peeled and crushed
grated zest of 1 lime
2 tablespoons lime juice
sea salt and cracked pepper
1/2 cup extra virgin olive oil

Place all ingredients except the olive oil in a food processor and pulse to a paste. Slowly add the oil while continuing to process.

MAKES 3/4 CUP

Stewart's Salty Sautéed Spuds

1.5kg floury potatoes, unpeeled
olive oil for roasting
salt

Thoroughly wash the potatoes. Cut them in half lengthways and place, cut side down, on absorbent kitchen paper to thoroughly dry. Slash the cut surface of the potatoes in a criss-cross pattern. Select a roasting pan just big enough to hold the potatoes and pour in enough olive oil to generously cover the bottom. Salt the cut surface of the potatoes and place them, cut-side down, in the olive oil. Roast the potatoes in an oven preheated to 210°C for 1 1/4 hours or until they are tender and crisp, and easily lift from the pan. Do not disturb the potatoes during cooking.

SERVES 6–8

Tomato Sauce

To vary the sauce simply add sprigs of fresh herbs, such as basil, thyme, oregano and rosemary, while it simmers.

2 tablespoons olive oil
2 cloves garlic, peeled and chopped
1 large onion, peeled and finely chopped
4 x 400g cans tomatoes in juice
sea salt and cracked pepper
1/2 teaspoon sugar
1 bay leaf

In a large saucepan heat the olive oil and fry the garlic and onion over a low heat until soft. Add the tomatoes, seasonings, sugar and bay leaf and simmer gently for 20 minutes. Allow to cool and remove the bay leaf and herb sprigs if used.

MAKES 6 CUPS

Char Roast Tomatoes and Onions with Rosemary

This colourful dish is great for barbecues because it can be prepared ahead of time and quickly reheated in the oven.

2 red onions
2 brown onions
2 tablespoons olive oil
4 tablespoons balsamic vinegar
sea salt and freshly ground black pepper
1 tablespoon fresh rosemary
4 tomatoes, halved
brown sugar
sprigs fresh rosemary to garnish

Cut the onions in half top to bottom. Peel each onion half, leaving the root attached to keep the onion intact. Combine the olive oil, balsamic vinegar, salt and pepper in the bottom of a roasting pan. Place the onions cut side down in the pan and sprinkle the rosemary over. Cover with aluminium foil and roast the onions in an oven preheated to 180°C for 20 minutes. Finish the cooking by grilling on an oiled barbecue over a medium heat until lightly charred.

Place the tomatoes skin side down on a medium–hot oiled barbecue grill. Season with salt, pepper and a pinch of brown sugar on each half. Grill for about 4 minutes, until lightly charred on the cut side, then turn to cook the other side.

Arrange the barbecued onions and tomatoes cut side up on a serving platter garnished with fresh rosemary sprigs.

SERVES 6–8

Susie's bean stew

Susie's Bean Stew

Wonderfully aromatic as it cooks, rich and tasty to eat, this wonderful accompaniment for barbecue meats can also be eaten warm or cold on bruschetta or fresh country bread.

3 cloves garlic, peeled and crushed
6 tablespoons olive oil
500g French beans, trimmed (or sliced flat beans)
1 cup fresh flat-leaf parsley, finely chopped
$^{1}/_{2}$–$^{3}/_{4}$ cup fresh dill, finely chopped
4–5 cups canned tomatoes in juice, finely chopped
sea salt and freshly ground black pepper
pinch of sugar

Fry the garlic in the olive oil over a low heat until soft and aromatic. Add the beans and cook for a further 5 minutes. Stir in the herbs, tomatoes, salt and pepper, and sugar. Simmer gently for 1 hour with the lid on, stirring occasionally.

SERVES 6

Sliced Summer Fruits in Palm Sugar Syrup

In this refreshing way to finish a barbecue meal use a selection of firm, ripe summer fruits such as nectarines, peaches, apricots, bananas, mangos and pawpaws.

200g palm sugar, grated
3/4 cup water
3/4 cup orange juice
2 tablespoons brown sugar
ripe summer fruits (nectarines, peaches, apricots, bananas, mangos, pawpaws)
300ml clotted cream or ice cream
Vanilla Sugar (see page 67)

To make the syrup, melt the palm sugar in a heavy-based saucepan over a low heat. As it dissolves, slowly add the water and orange juice and stir to combine. When the palm sugar is dissolved add the brown sugar, simmer gently for 5 minutes and allow to cool.

Prepare the fruit and cut it into pieces that can easily be picked up by hand. Dip into the cooled syrup and barbecue on a preheated grill over a medium–high heat until the syrup caramelises and the fruit softens. Place the grilled fruit in a serving dish and pour the remaining syrup over. Serve with clotted cream flavoured with Vanilla Sugar.

SERVES 6–8

Sliced summer fruits in palm sugar syrup

Lime Pudding Pots

This dessert has a refreshing tart flavour perfect for finishing a meal.

4 tablespoons softened butter
1/4 cup caster sugar
4 tablespoons self-raising flour
6 tablespoons lime juice
1 1/2 tablespoons grated lime zest
1 cup milk
4 eggs, separated
icing sugar for serving
mascarpone cheese or whipped cream for serving

Cream the butter and sugar together until pale. Stir in the flour and lime juice and zest. Add the milk and egg yolks and beat well to combine. In a separate bowl beat the egg whites until they form soft peaks. Gently fold the egg whites into the pudding mixture. Pour the mixture into eight 150ml ramekins and bake in an oven preheated to 160°C for 20–25 minutes or until the tops are golden. The bottom of the pudding should still be gooey. Dust the tops with icing sugar and serve with a little mascarpone or whipped cream.

MAKES 8

Dreamy Hokey-pokey Ice Cream and Caramel Sauce

1/2 cup sugar
4 tablespoons golden syrup
2 teaspoons bicarbonate of soda
1 litre good quality store-bought French vanilla ice cream
a little Caramel Sauce (see below)

To make the hokey-pokey, bring the sugar and golden syrup to the boil slowly, stirring constantly. Simmer gently over a very low heat for 4 minutes. Remove from the heat and immediately add the bicarbonate of soda, stirring it in quickly as it froths up in the saucepan. Pour immediately into a greased cake tin and allow it to harden and cool. Break it into small chunks.

Take the ice cream out of the freezer and allow it to soften just enough that you can stir it. Stir the hokey-pokey through the ice cream, then return it to the freezer to harden again.

Serve a couple of scoops of ice cream in a glass drizzled with a soupçon of Caramel Sauce and, if you fancy, biscotti.

SERVES 8

Caramel Sauce

1 1/4 cups sugar
100ml water
150ml cream

Dissolve the sugar in the water in a heavy-bottomed saucepan over a low heat, stirring occasionally. Bring to a gentle simmer and allow the syrup to caramelise to a dark golden colour. While it caramelises, warm the cream in a small saucepan until tepid. Remove the caramelised sugar from the heat and stir in the cream until it is smooth.

MAKES 1 1/2 CUPS

Double Chocolate Espresso Tart

This is very decadent, and absolutely divine. Serve it with fresh summer berries and runny cream – and remember that a little bit goes a long way.

PASTRY

150g plain flour, sifted
1 tablespoon caster sugar
1 tablespoon cocoa powder
100g cold butter, cubed
1 large egg yolk
cold water

FILLING

300g dark cooking chocolate
100g butter
50ml cream
50ml cold double-strength espresso coffee
4 eggs plus 1 yolk
100g caster sugar

To make the pastry, place the flour, caster sugar, cocoa and butter in a food processor and process until the mixture resembles fine breadcrumbs. Add the egg yolk and continue to process, adding enough cold water to bind the dough together. Remove the mixture to a lightly floured board and form the dough into a ball. Wrap in plastic wrap and refrigerate for 20 minutes.

On a lightly floured board roll out the pastry and use it to line a lightly greased, loose-bottomed, fluted 25cm tart tin. Prick the base with a fork. Cover the pastry with aluminium foil weighed down with dried beans or rice, then bake blind in an oven preheated to 170°C for 15 minutes. Remove the beans or rice and foil and return the tart to the oven at 170°C for a further 10–15 minutes to firm the pastry.

To make the filling, melt the chocolate and butter with the cream and espresso in the microwave on low power. Beat the eggs, the extra egg yolk and sugar together until thick and pale. In a double boiler or a metal bowl over a pot of gently simmering water, continue to whisk the eggs and sugar until the texture firms a little. Keep the heat low to avoid scrambling the egg. Remove from the heat, fold in the chocolate mixture and pour into the tart shell. Bake in an oven preheated to 180°C for 10–15 minutes or until the filling rises, firms and springs back to the touch.

SERVES 8–10

glossary

Blanching
This technique involves plunging food (usually vegetables or fruit) into boiling water for about 10 seconds and then into cold water to stop the cooking process. It's used to firm the flesh and loosen skins, and to heighten and set the colour and flavour of food.

Burghul wheat
A staple of the Middle East, burghul is the steamed, dried and crushed wheat that gives the tender, chewy texture to tabbouleh.

Dukkah
Dukkah is a coarsely ground mixture of toasted hazelnuts, toasted sesame seeds, coriander seeds and sometimes mustard seeds, sea salt, coarsely ground black pepper and oil. It can be eaten as a snack, sprinkled over oil-toasted pita bread, tossed with vegetables or sprinkled over grilled lamb or fish. It's easy to make your own but commercial preparations are readily available from most good supermarkets and specialty food stores.

Dutch cocoa powder
This cocoa is treated with an alkali that neutralises the cocoa's natural acidity. It can be found at specialty food stores.

Fromage blanc
Very similar to quark, fromage blanc is a skimmed milk cheese available in many supermarkets.

Ganache
This rich chocolate icing is made from semi-sweet chocolate and cream heated and stirred together until the chocolate melts.

Haloumi cheese
Originating in Cyprus, this hardish cheese is made from a stretched curd and has a texture rather like mozzarella. It is made from sheep's, cow's or goat's milk (or a blend) and is eaten uncooked or cut into chunks and grilled or fried. Haloumi cheese can be found in specialty food stores and some supermarkets.

Hapuku
Also known as groper, hapuku, with its meaty, solid flesh and robust flavour, is often described as a 'fish eater's fish'. It is available whole, filleted or in steaks.

Hoisin sauce
This thick, reddish-brown, sweet and spicy sauce is made from soy beans, garlic, chilli and various spices. It is widely used in Chinese cuisine as a condiment or a flavouring agent in meat, poultry and fish dishes and is stocked by most supermarkets and Asian stores.

Kabayaki Dory
Hot-smoked John Dory fillets are basted with an oriental dressing and sealed into 200g packets. Only available in New Zealand, Kabayaki Dory can be found in the fish section of many supermarkets.

Kaffir lime leaves
Used extensively in Thai cuisine, kaffir lime is a native of South-east Asia. The leaves are extremely fragrant and often added to soups whole, shredded or torn. Cut into strips they can be added to salads, dressings, marinades and curries.

Orzo
Meaning 'barley' in Italian, orzo is a tiny rice-shaped pasta about the size of a pine nut. It's great in soups and salads or as a substitute for rice.

Palm sugar
Indian and Thai cooking often call for palm sugar's sweet, winy fragrance and toffee flavour. Also known as jaggery, it is a dark, coarse, unrefined sugar made from either the sap of the palm tree or from sugar cane juice. Palm sugar is mainly sold in a solid cake that has to be grated or melted before use, but it can also be found with a soft honey butter texture. It is most easily purchased from Asian supermarkets and specialty food stores.

Pancetta
This Italian bacon, used to flavour sauces, pasta dishes, forcemeats and vegetables, is cured with salt but not smoked. It is available from specialty

food stores and some supermarkets.

Pangritata

Originating in Italy, pangritata is simply breadcrumbs fried or toasted in garlic oil.

Pecorino cheese

An Italian cheese made from sheep's milk, pecorino is a hard, dry cheese used for grating and cooking. It can be used to replace parmesan. Many supermarkets and specialty food stores supply it.

Prosciutto

The Italian word for ham, 'prosciutto' is a term broadly used to describe ham that has been seasoned, cured with salt and air-dried without being smoked. The meat is then pressed into a firm dense texture. Purchase prosciutto from most good delicatessens and some supermarkets. It is usually sold cut in very thin slices laid flat. Although it's at its best eaten in this form it is also great to use grilled crisp in salads or added at the last minute to cooked foods such as pasta or vegetables. Parma ham is a true prosciutto.

Snapper

This species of sea bream has a medium-dense texture and is sold whole or filleted.

Tarakihi

This medium-firm white fish is great for baking whole but is also available filleted.

Verjuice

Verjuice (or verjus) is the juice of unripe grapes, crushed and strained. It's excellent for deglazing pans or used in vinaigrettes and sauces or with fish and poultry. Usually made from grapes that are high in acid and low in sugar, it gives a light, fresh acidity that is gentler than vinegar. It moves in and out of culinary fashion but is available at specialty food stores and some supermarkets.

Vermicelli

Vermicelli is Italian for 'little worms'. In the culinary sense it refers to very thin strands of pasta.

Whitebait

New Zealand whitebait are quite different from overseas species. They are tiny, clear, worm-like fish that turn white on cooking. They are a seasonal delicacy caught in tidal river estuaries in the spring.

NZ/AUSTRALIA	US	GREAT BRITAIN
Beetroot	beet	beetroot
Capsicum	bell pepper	pepper
Caster sugar	superfine sugar	caster sugar
Cornflour	cornstarch	cornflour
Cream (NZ)	whipping cream	whipping cream
Eggplant	eggplant	aubergine
Ginger Nuts	Ginger Snaps	Ginger Nuts
Golden syrup	corn syrup	golden syrup
Grill	broil	grill
Icing sugar	confectioner's sugar	icing sugar
Minced beef	ground beef	minced beef
Plain flour	all-purpose flour	plain flour
Prawn	shrimp	prawn
Rock melon	cantaloupe	cantaloupe or musk melon
Self-raising flour	self-rising flour	self-raising flour
Sultanas	seedless white raisins	sultanas
Tasty cheese	cheddar or jack cheese	cheddar cheese
Tomato paste	tomato paste	tomato purée
Zucchini	zucchini	courgette

weights & measures

Abbreviations

g	gram
kg	kilogram
mm	millimetre
cm	centimetre
ml	millilitre
°C	degrees Celsius

Weight conversions

NZ METRIC	IMPERIAL/US
25g	1 oz
50g	2 oz
75g	3 oz
100g	3 1/2 oz
125g	4 1/2 oz
150g	5 oz
175g	6 oz
200g	7 oz
225g	8 oz
250g	9 oz
275g	9 1/2 oz
300g	10 1/2 oz
325g	11 1/2 oz
350g	12 1/2 oz
375g	13 oz
400g	14 oz
450g	16 oz (1 lb)
500g	17 1/2 oz
750g	26 1/2 oz
1 kg	35 oz (2 1/4 lb)

Length conversions

METRIC	IMPERIAL/US
0.5cm (5mm)	1/4 inch
1cm	1/2 inch
2.5cm	1 inch
5cm	2 inches
10cm	4 inches
20cm	8 inches
30cm	12 inches (1 foot)

Liquid conversions

NZ METRIC	IMPERIAL	US
5ml (1 teaspoon)	1/4 fl oz	1 teaspoon
15ml (1 tablespoon)	1/2 fl oz	1 tablespoon
30ml (1/8 cup)	1 fl oz	1/8 cup
60ml (1/4 cup)	2 fl oz	1/4 cup
125ml (1/2 cup)	4 fl oz	1/2 cup
150ml	5 fl oz (1/4 pint)	2/3 cup
175ml	6 fl oz	3/4 cup
250ml (1 cup)	8 fl oz	1 cup (1/2 pint)
300ml	10 fl oz (1/2 pint)	1 1/4 cups
375ml	12 fl oz	1 1/2 cups
500ml (2 cups)	16 fl oz	2 cups (1 pint)
600ml	20 fl oz (1 pint)	2 1/2 cups

NB The Australian metric tablespoon measures 20ml

Temperature conversions

CELSIUS	FAHRENHEIT	GAS
100°C	225°F	1/4
125°C	250°F	1/2
150°C	300°F	2
160°C	325°F	3
170°C	325°F	3
180°C	350°F	4
190°C	375°F	5
200°C	400°F	6
210°C	425°F	7
220°C	425°F	7
230°C	450°F	8
250°C	500°F	9

Cake tin sizes

METRIC	IMPERIAL/US
15cm	6 inches
18cm	7 inches
20cm	8 inches
23cm	9 inches
25cm	10 inches
28cm	11 inches

index

t

v

w

y

z

acknowledgements

Thanks so much to my husband, Stewart, for his consistent support and discerning palate, and to my son, Oliver, who sat on the bench, giving instructions and operating the mini prep while I cooked.

Many creative people contributed their time and talents to help make this beautiful book. Thanks to my friends Susie and Roger MacDonald for their help, hospitality, home and Waiheke locations; Emma and Amanda for clever props and for Nero the dog; Kirsten and Marcella for their enthusiasm and time, and John for the antique dinghy and endless supply of fresh fish; John Waring and Sam for the Weber; Lyn and Julie at *Cuisine* magazine for their understanding and extended deadlines; and Jeff Thompson for my treasured piece of corrugated iron.

Thanks also to Alison Dench for her refined editing skill; designer Christine Hansen for her exceptional creative talent, and a special thank you to Ian Batchelor, whose food images never fail to inspire me.

Thanks to Renée Lang, Belinda Cooke and the rest of the New Holland team for giving me the opportunity to publish my first cookbook – a totally enlightening but pleasant experience.

suppliers

Elpie Burt, Piper Antiques, Richmond Road, Ponsonby, Auckland
Country Road Homewares, Newmarket, Auckland
Albertine – plates and crockery, Ponsonby Road, Auckland
Jane Gilmore, Southern Clams Ltd
Candice Reinecke, New Zealand King Salmon Co Ltd
Maureen Fitzgerald, Flying Fingers Secretarial Services, Ponsonby, Auckland